Mending Your Broken Heart

A Survival Kit

*A self-directed recovery plan to help put the pieces
together again after your relationship has ended*

Ann McGill, PhD & Glynis Wilson, MA

Detselig Enterprises Ltd.
Calgary, Alberta, Canada

Mending Your Broken Heart

© 1994 Ann McGill and Glynis Wilson

Canadian Cataloguing in Publication Data

McGill, Ann Carley.
  Mending your broken heart

Includes bibliographical references.
ISBN 1-55059-091-X

   1. Separation (Psychology)   2. Grief   I. Wilson, Glynis,
[date]-   II. Title.
BF575.G7M33   1994   158'.2   C94-910460-4

Publisher's Data

Detselig Enterprises Ltd.
210, 1220 Kensington Road NW
Calgary, Alberta T2N 3P5

Cover design by Dean MacDonald

SAN 115-0324   ISBN 1-55059-091-X

Printed in Canada

To my mother Emily,
who did so well
in mending
her own broken heart.
– Ann

To my sister Andrea,
whose heart is whole
and stronger than ever.
With love and admiration.
– Glynis

Acknowledgments

We would like to thank both Dr. Shannon Fleming and Dr. Shirley Shantz who read the manuscript in progress and made valuable suggestions. Thanks also to Lorelei Kelliher who worked long hours typing the manuscript. We also thank our fine editor, Sherry Wilson McEwen, for her assistance in preparing the manuscript for publication. Our husbands, Neil and Paul, for providing ongoing support and encouragement for which we are deeply grateful. And finally, we would like to thank Paul Boultbee for his invaluable work as agent and research assistant.

Detselig Enterprises Ltd. appreciates the financial support for our 1994 publishing program, provided by the Department of Canadian Heritage, Canada Council and the Alberta Foundation for the Arts, a beneficiary of the Lottery Fund of the Government of Alberta.

Other books in Detselig's **Lifeline** series:

Opening the Doors to Canadian Medical Schools
Reflections on Relaxation
Backyard Trampolining
Boot Camp: Basic Training For Your Dog
Cut Auto Repair Costs

Foreword

From all of us who have known the pain of a broken heart . . . THANK YOU, Ann and Glynis. Your book unfolds like a gentle hand guiding us through the mists of this incredibly vulnerable time, encouraging us to reconnect with a sense of our **self** and a belief in our **future.**

Mending Your Broken Heart is a journey into an emotional world many of us find ourselves unprepared to handle. Ann and Glynis weave years of human and psychological wisdom into a clear, straightforward and practical guide for stepping through this world. They provide a framework for understanding the difficult and often overwhelming experience of initial loss . . . then allow you to select and work on those issues specific to your personal journey. Information deepens your awareness of patterns that block well-being, while self-assessment procedures, guided exercises and daily monitoring schedules help you establish new "recipes for living" that nourish body, mind and soul.

As you walk the well-designed path of this book, you come to realize that while the heart feels broken, the spirit has only bent to help the heart mend, and eventually both will reawaken and open to the new forms of life that are waiting to enter.

Dr. Shannon Fleming
PhD Psychology
Priddis, Alberta

Sections

Introduction

Mending Your Broken Heart is designed for people who have separated from an important romantic partner. You may have chosen to leave the relationship, your partner may have been the one to decide or perhaps the decision was mutual. No matter what the circumstances, you are probably experiencing a lot of pain.

This is a difficult time. You're faced with many changes and you may find yourself looking for something or someone to help you through it. We don't offer a magic cure, but this book will help you find your way through the pain and help you make sense of your new future.

How to Use this Book

Mending Your Broken Heart is divided into three parts: **The Issues, Weekly Activities and Reflections,** and **Putting it All Together.** The first two parts are for your use right away. You may want to save Part Three for a little later.

Part One: The Issues

In this section, we've provided information about several issues you may be struggling with. Not all will apply to you, so select only the ones that seem relevant. We chose the order we think makes most sense, but you'll know best what you want to read about. Feel free to read the sections in any order. In several cases, we've provided an assessment to help you get a general sense of how you're doing with a particular issue. These assessments are not meant to be conclusive – they are intended to help you begin to sort things out.

We have covered the central issues involved in ending a relationship. You may find that you want to explore a particular issue in greater depth, so we have provided a **Resources** section at the back of the book. Many of the books listed there should be available at a public library or in a bookstore.

Part Two: Weekly Activities and Reflections

This part is self-directed. First, you are asked to set reasonable weekly goals designed to look after your body and your soul. There's also a place to do some writing about your feelings. These activities and reflections are a key part of the recovery process.

Set aside time each week to work on Part Two. Sunday afternoons or evenings are often good times. Try to find a place where you won't be disturbed for at least half an hour. If you have children, be sure to find some time when they are asleep or out or unlikely to disturb you. In the weekly goal-setting section of Part Two, we've listed a whole range of activities to keep body and soul together. Not every activity will appeal to you, but we've tried to include something for everyone. Keep in mind that depression often limits your interests. If nothing appeals to you, set goals anyway and then work on achieving them. One important way of fighting depression is to get active and involved in life.

Many of the activities we've suggested are low- or no-cost. Others will be more expensive. Choose activities to fit your pocket book. And whether you can afford it or not, avoid spending a great deal of money. Comfort spending, like comfort eating, can create its own set of problems.

The **Reflections** section of Part Two asks you to do some writing in order to make sense of what you are feeling right now. You don't have to write a lot, but do get something down. Remember, the writing is for your eyes only. Don't worry about how it sounds; don't worry about grammar or spelling or punctuation. The important part of the exercise is the thinking that you do before, during and after the writing.

One suggestion: when you're writing about the past, you may find you focus only on the good times in the relationship. If so, spend some time reflecting about the other times. And similarly, if you're stuck on the bad stuff, try looking for other perspectives. Thinking about what you miss and what you don't miss may be helpful in getting started. One of the main reasons for examining the past is to learn for the future. Try thinking about what you would like to change so that you can avoid repeating your past.

Part Three: Putting It All Together

The final part of the book asks you to set some long-term goals – to decide where you want to go from here. As we mentioned before, you may want to save this part for a time when you are feeling able to focus positively on the future. Guard against a desire to rush forward into the future before resolving issues from the past. Right now, allow yourself to grieve, to experience and come to terms with the pain.

What if you stop using the book for awhile?

Sometimes it happens. For a week or two or longer, you find yourself unable to do the weekly **Activities and Reflections** outlined in Part Two. That's okay. Ideally, you would do it every week, but we know that sometimes you may feel you're too busy or depressed or angry. As soon as you can, start it up again. Make the effort even if it seems overwhelming. The important thing is to continue in your attempts to deal with how you feel and to move forward.

What if you return briefly to the relationship?

Sometimes it's hard to bring a relationship to an end. There always seem to be so many loose ends, so many things tying you to your partner. So if you do patch things up briefly only to find that it's still not going to work, remember that you're not alone. Many others follow this same route. You'll probably feel bad that it didn't work, but it doesn't mean you're a failure. It just means you tried something that wasn't meant to be.

What should you do? As soon as possible, return to the weekly **Activities and Reflections** outlined in Part Two. As you write about the experience of returning to the relationship, look for what you can learn from it.

And so . . .

And so now you're ready to begin using this book. We wish you well on your journey – through grieving and healing to recovery and new-found strength.

Part One: The Issues

Part One: The Issues provides introductions to several issues you may be working through right now. Be selective – read about the topics that interest you, in any order. If a topic is of particular interest to you, the **Resources** section provides a list of books that go into more detail.

Contents

Figure 1. The Grief Model

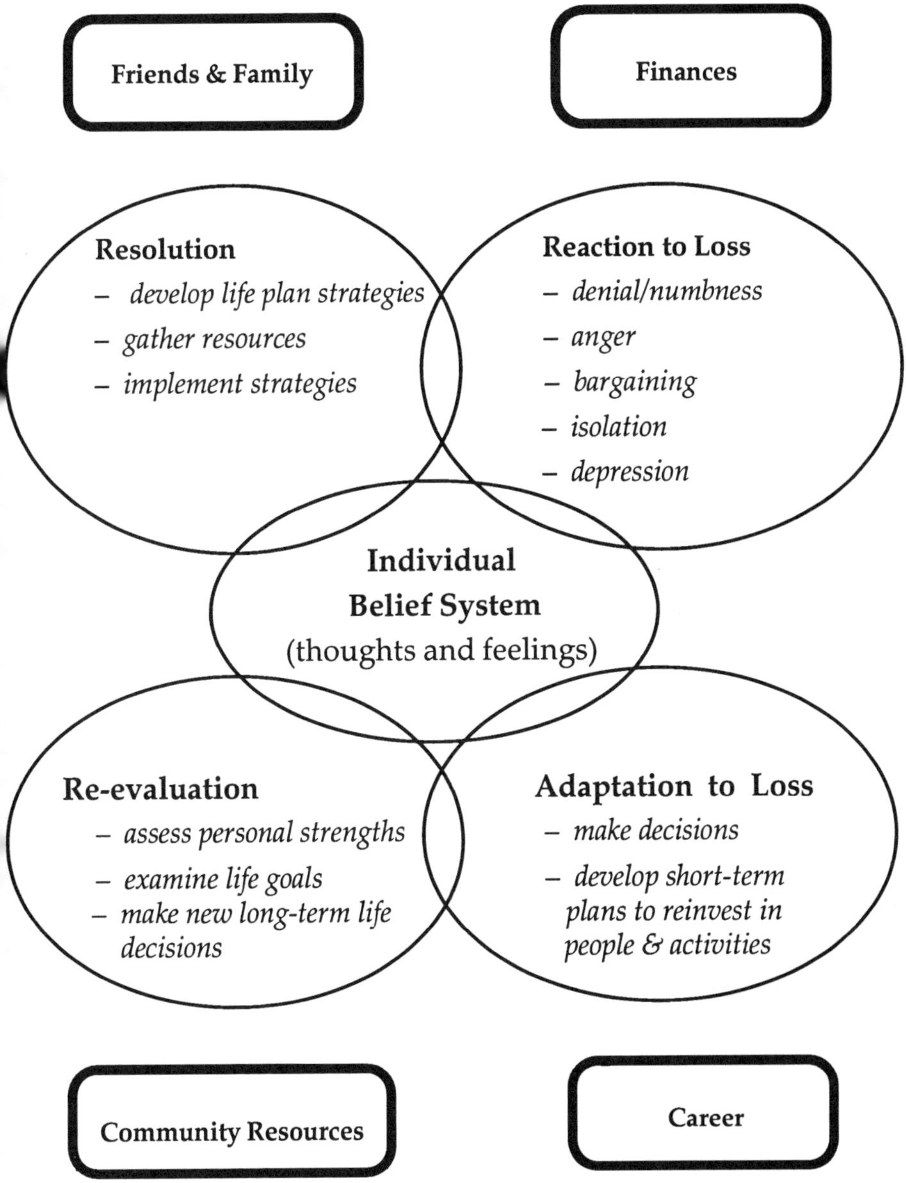

Friends & Family

Finances

Resolution
- *develop life plan strategies*
- *gather resources*
- *implement strategies*

Reaction to Loss
- *denial/numbness*
- *anger*
- *bargaining*
- *isolation*
- *depression*

**Individual
Belief System**
(thoughts and feelings)

Re-evaluation
- *assess personal strengths*
- *examine life goals*
- *make new long-term life decisions*

Adaptation to Loss
- *make decisions*
- *develop short-term plans to reinvest in people & activities*

Community Resources

Career

The Process of Loss

Figure 1 on the previous page shows the process of loss as it occurs for many people. In the centre is the individual's own belief system – his or her thoughts and feelings, which have evolved over time. This belief system is at the core of the loss process.

You will notice several large circles in the diagram which represent the phases of an individual's experience of loss. Research suggests that people go through certain stages in coming to terms with any crisis they face. The circles overlap to indicate that this process does not progress in a rigid and linear fashion. As well, the experience of loss sometimes significantly affects a person's core beliefs.

The initial reaction to loss includes numbness, anger, depression and feelings of isolation. Then adaptation to the loss begins: the individual starts to rebuild his or her life, making short-term decisions and moving forward. As a result of developing new and perhaps unfamiliar ways of living, the person examines the attitudes and values that have shaped his or her life. He or she may develop long-term plans to achieve a new set of goals.

The process of loss can be seen as circular, with no beginning or end. Most individuals move back and forth in the process. Just when they think they have it all together, something occurs to catapult them back to the beginning. Typically, these are temporary setbacks, followed by significant leaps forward.

Other factors affect the person as he or she copes with this process, and while being intricately linked with the individual, they are outside the self. These external factors include family and friends, finances, community resources and career.

This model attempts to take a complicated human process and put it into an understandable form. You may find that the model does not precisely match what is happening in your life. In many ways, however, it will parallel your experience.

The Initial Experience of Grief

Grief is the natural reaction to loss. If you lose an important person in your life, you must work through grief in order to come to terms with this loss. Every person's grief takes a different path, but initially most people experience numbness and shock followed by acute pain.

Numbness or Shock

The process of grieving may begin with a period of numbness or shock. This is nature's way of buffering you initially from the full impact of your loss, giving you time to gather your coping resources. During this time, you may feel dazed and almost detached from reality. Some people describe this as "going through the motions."

The Next Stage: Feelings

As the numbness wears off, you will come face-to-face with your loss and begin to experience the pain of grief. At this time, you feel a wide and probably confusing range of emotions, including intense sadness, despair and perhaps even relief. You may also feel anxiety, fear or even panic about what the future holds. Because no one can experience the pain of separation in exactly the same way, you may feel a sense of isolation and loneliness. And you will almost certainly feel anger and resentment that this had to happen to you and your relationship. Regardless of the circumstances of the loss, you may also feel guilt – for your part in ending the relationship, for things done or not done. In fact, you may feel that your emotions are out of control.

Day-to-Day

Day-to-day activities often become difficult as the numbness wears off. Your head is probably filled with thoughts and memories of your partner. Consequently, you may lose your ability to think clearly and concentrate fully. Short-term memory may become impaired. Because your pattern of living has been radically disrupted, you may also become very disorganized.

Because your thoughts are in the past, you may have difficulty finding motivation for the present. The absence of someone important means the loss of a way of life and a dream for the future. As a result, present and future will have diminished in meaning. Sleep becomes difficult and dreaming may increase dramatically. And as you become more fatigued, you may also experience a decrease in both your appetite and your general sense of health and well-being. Because of the range and intensity of your emotions right now, you may cry a great deal.

As you go about daily business, you will likely feel restless, unable to settle on any one activity. You may, for example, start to make a bed and wander off to do something else before the task is completed.

Dealing with the Initial Pain of Grief

All of these feelings and experiences are a normal part of grief. They may be distressing, but take comfort in the knowledge that they won't last forever. In the meantime, it is most important to allow yourself time to grieve.

The following activities should help:

- Talk about your thoughts and feelings with someone who is sympathetic and understanding.
- Allow yourself to cry.
- Set aside time each day to concentrate on your loss. This will help you focus on the present for the rest of the day.
- Gather resources to help you cope, including people (friends and relatives) and information sources (books, articles, etc.).
- Accept invitations from friends and family.
- Make lists to help you organize and remember what you must do.

Note: Working through this book is another way to begin coping with the pain of your loss. Good for you!

Previous Losses

The loss of a love may rekindle issues related to a loss or losses experienced in the past. Even if these previous losses were dealt with as fully as possible, strong feelings may come back into your present situation. It's important to know that this is a normal reaction.

Feelings about a previous loss can certainly add to your present grief. If the past loss was particularly difficult (for example, the premature loss of a parent or sibling), then painful feelings may recur fairly easily. If, on the other hand, the loss was expected (for example, the loss of a grandparent), then your feelings were probably easier to resolve and may have less impact now.

Whatever the circumstances of the previous loss, accept the feelings you are having now. They are normal.

When He/She Leaves You for Someone Else

The catalyst for the end of a loving relationship is often a third person. Because many people believe that even a bad relationship is better than none at all, a relationship in trouble will often continue until someone else arrives on the scene.

If you were left for another man or woman, you are probably feeling a lot of pain right now. It is difficult to think of your ex-partner happily settled in another relationship while you suffer alone. You may be wondering if your ex-partner ever truly loved you, given how easily he or she, "in the arms of another," has forgotten you. You will feel particularly distressed if you believe that the new partner is younger, more attractive, more talented, more fun and so on. And finally, if you have children, you may worry that they will want to spend time in a "happy family group" – with them – instead of with you, a lonely, unhappy parent.

While you are powerless to control the behavior of others, you *can* choose how you think about this situation. First, if you must compare yourself to the new partner, don't focus only on your weaknesses – be sure to recognize your many strengths. Better still, don't make comparisons at all. Each of you is a unique human being.

Sometimes it's easier to blame the "other person" for the end of the relationship than it is to accept that you and your ex-partner must both bear some of the responsibility. Try to avoid "blaming" him or her. No one person is totally responsible for the ending of a relationship – or the beginning of another.

If you worry about losing your children to the "happy couple," remember the strength of shared history and family feelings. Allow the feelings to motivate you to work on your relationship with your children. Children (and adults) thrive on time, attention, involvement and love.

If you live in fear of encountering the "other person," you have a couple of choices. Grit your teeth, recognizing that if you do meet, it will not be a total disaster; in fact, the meeting will give you an opportunity to demonstrate how cool and collected you can be (at least on the outside). Or you can do everything in your power to avoid the situation by staying away from the places where the other person tends to be. Make the choice that feels right.

While it's natural to feel angry that your ex-partner is with someone else, this emotion doesn't have to consume your life. Find ways to get on with your own life because you deserve to find happiness too.

When You Do the Leaving

If you are the one who made the decision to end the relationship, you are probably experiencing a lot of guilt right now. And any relief you feel may only increase your guilt. No wonder you feel like you're on a roller coaster.

Even though you made the final decision, don't blame yourself for the fact that the relationship is over. Just as it takes two to make a healthy relationship, partners must both take partial responsibility for its demise. If you thought that it was important to leave, then the relationship was already in trouble. And if your partner claims that everything was fine, remember the pain you felt as you were making your decision. That pain wasn't experienced within a "perfectly fine" situation.

Sometimes when you have made the decision to leave, your partner will do everything possible to convince you to stay. This may include unusually loving and generous gestures. Even though these actions could increase your guilt about leaving, you may also feel angry because they are "too little, too late."

The demise of a relationship can batter self-esteem. If your partner is urging you to stay, you may be tempted to agree because it feels so good to be loved. Remember, though, that unhealthy relationships contribute to low self-esteem. If these loving gestures and pleas to stay don't rekindle your love, then perhaps it's best to let it go.

Guilt could also prevent you from ending the relationship cleanly. In attempting to be kind, you may try to let your partner down "gently" – agreeing to meet frequently and talking on the phone even when you don't want to. This strategy rarely works. The pain is not lessened for your partner; it's simply prolonged for both of you.

Anxiety and Panic Attacks

Anxiety

Most of us experience vague feelings of discomfort and uneasiness from time to time. When dealing with a major change in life, anxiety may occur more frequently. Sometimes you will understand how the loss you've experienced has contributed to your anxiety, while at other times there doesn't seem to be a specific reason for the anxious feeling. In either case, anxious feelings are never pleasant.

Anxiety is triggered by thoughts. When we're unsure about the future, we often start to imagine all kinds of negative possibilities. As we visualize these scenarios, our bodies react as if these events were really going to happen and we become afraid. As a result, we begin to experience a wide range of mild to moderate physical symptoms, including shortness of breath, rapid heartbeat, nausea, abdominal pain, fatigue and feelings of weakness.

Panic Attacks

If, on the other hand, you have episodes of acute fear which go beyond mild to moderate anxiety, you may be experiencing panic attacks. All of a sudden, perhaps for no apparent reason, you are overwhelmed by feelings of impending doom. You may also experience a sense of unreality. Physical symptoms which accompany panic attacks are more severe than those experienced when feeling anxious. You may have difficulty breathing; your hands may tremble; your legs may feel like rubber; your heart may be racing. Many people who have experienced panic attacks report that they were sure they were dying or going crazy.

Although they may seem unexpected, panic attacks don't come out of the blue. When you have lived with high stress for an extended period with no way to relieve it, your body actually speeds up the production of stress chemicals. You may also have been physically run down – eating poorly, losing sleep and so on. People who are physically and psychologically fragile are often more vulnerable to panic attacks.

The panic attacks are also triggered by thoughts and can occur with little or no warning. These thoughts set in motion a chemical reaction which causes the symptoms of panic: adrenaline, which is sent into the bloodstream, causes breathing and heart rates to increase. At the same time, there may be overwhelming feelings of fear or dread. Because there is no reasonable way to get rid of the energy produced by the adrenaline, the individual experiences the symptoms without being able to relieve them.

It is important to note that not everyone reacts to high stress in this way. Your own reaction to grief may not include panic attacks, although you will almost certainly experience feelings of anxiety at some point during the process.

What can you do about anxiety and panic attacks?

- If thoughts trigger anxiety and panic attacks, one of the most effective ways to help yourself is to alter your thoughts. One way to do this is to use thought-stopping and self-talk (see page 42). By changing what you tell yourself about yourself and your future, you can decrease your anxiety quite dramatically.

- Examine your life to identify your worries and fears. Work out strategies to reduce or eliminate these stressors.

- Include relaxation exercises (such as yoga, meditation, self-hypnosis, deep muscle relaxation) in your daily routine (see page 39).

- Make sure your diet is well-balanced and healthy (see page 31).

- Make sure you are getting adequate rest and sleep (see page 26)

- Exercise on a regular basis (see page 35).

- Interacting regularly with close, trustworthy friends at this time will help ease feelings of anxiety (see pages 56 to 59 if you are interested in attending to or extending your social network).

- Consult your physician.

Note: A healthy lifestyle and a sense of emotional well-being are two of the most important factors that affect anxiety and stress levels. Throughout this book, many of the activities are designed to address these issues.

Are You Experiencing Anxiety or Panic Attacks?

It's sometimes difficult to determine the difference between strong feelings of anxiety and a full-blown panic attack. You may want to use the list below to determine which you are experiencing. Check all that apply.

My feelings of anxiety seem to come on suddenly for no apparent reason. They have been accompanied by:

_____ shortness of breath

_____ sweating

_____ dizziness, faintness or unsteadiness

_____ nausea

_____ fear of going crazy, dying or losing control

_____ a racing heart or palpitations

_____ feeling choked or smothered

_____ mild to moderate chest pain

_____ shaking or trembling

_____ cold or hot flashes

_____ numbness or tingling

_____ feeling detached or unreal

These are some of the symptoms of panic attacks. If you checked a number of them, ask a doctor or mental health professional for assistance. There is no reason for you to suffer alone as there are increasing avenues open to people suffering from these symptoms.

Addictions and Grief

The loss of a relationship nearly always produces some anxiety – and many human beings have difficulty dealing with anxiety. We search for ways to reduce it, to make these feelings more manageable. Some choose to take prescription or non-prescription drugs, to smoke cigarettes or to drink alcohol. Use of these substances may start out by helping us feel better. The alcohol or narcotic effect creates a chemical high or a feeling of well-being. It deadens the pain.

The desire to suppress pain is natural and may sometimes even be necessary. Prescription drugs taken right after a loss may be useful. They may allow you the time to marshall your resources until you are prepared to deal with the reality of loss. If you become dependent on them, they begin to cause more problems than they solve. They no longer provide an effective way of coping.

One of the problems is that the dependency may prevent you from dealing with the reality of your situation. You may become addicted to the substance that has deadened your pain. As a result, your life will actually become more complicated and more difficult. The substances you are addicted to are often depressants which compound feelings of sadness. After a time, you may find yourself struggling with addiction instead of grief.

Not all addictions involve the abuse of substances such as drugs and alcohol. Activities can also become addictive. Excessive sleeping, eating, exercising and shopping, for example, can be used to deaden the pain. Some people use sex or overcrowd their social calender to avoid having to be alone and confronting the reality of their loss.

What to Do About Addictions

There are many ways to cope with an addiction. If you're going to try to deal with it on your own, these suggestions may be helpful:

- Gather as much information as you can about the addiction.

- Keep track of your addictive behaviors and find out what events or feelings trigger them.

- Discover what your addiction is doing for you and try to develop alternate ways of dealing with the problem.

- Decide what you can do to modify your behavior, make a conscious decision to modify it and follow through on this decision.

- Be sure to reward yourself when you are successful.

Another way of dealing with an addiction is to find help. You can choose a 12-step support group (e.g.: Alcoholics Anonymous, Narcotics Anonymous, Overeaters Anonymous) or a qualified professional, for example a psychologist, social worker, dietician. If you have a history of addictive behaviors, you will need help in order to deal effectively with your addiction – especially as you are also coping with grief.

Sleep Disturbances

People who are under a great deal of stress often have difficulty maintaining their regular sleep patterns. Some people find that they want to sleep all the time; they can hardly stay awake. More commonly, though, people suffer from insomnia. They have trouble falling asleep; they wake up in the middle of the night and have difficulty falling asleep again; or they may wake up extremely early and never get back to sleep. People often get into a vicious and frustrating cycle: the more they try to sleep, the less sleep they get and the less sleep they get, the harder they try.

Establishing Rituals

To break the cycle, try establishing a ritual before you settle down to sleep. At the same time each night – approximately an hour before turning the light out – begin to prepare for sleep. Some people find that listening to soft music is useful, followed by some other relaxing activity like reading a light book, drinking a mug of warm milk or soaking in a warm bath. These activities send your body a signal that this is a transition time between the activity of the day and the inactivity of sleep.

One thing to remember: these rituals will only work if you need sleep. If you sleep during the day, you need less sleep at night. When you're trying to break a pattern of sleep disruption, it's best to avoid daytime napping.

About Food

A light snack before bedtime can be helpful and is even a must for some people. Make sure that the snack is high in carbohydrates (crackers, toast). Avoid a lot of protein (meat or cheese) and stimulants such as sugar and caffeine (found in cocoa, chocolate and cola soft drinks as well as coffee and tea). That glass of warm milk may also help. An enzyme, released when the milk is heated, has been shown to promote sleep.

About Drugs

Sleeping pills are sometimes used for a short time to break a stubborn pattern of insomnia. If your doctor has recommended that you try sleeping pills for a short time, that's okay. You might also be tempted to use alcohol or other non-prescription drugs to help you get to sleep. Because they are depressants, these drugs often do work initially. Unfortunately, there are two problems with this solution. First, when the effects of the depressant wear off, you may wake up in the middle of the night and have more difficulty getting back to sleep. Second, even if you do sleep through the night, you are experiencing a drugged sleep which disrupts your normal rhythms. Ultimately, the solution can become a further problem.

Adjusting to Sleeping Alone

If you are used to sleeping with someone else, you may not be happy about sleeping alone. There are, however, some things that can help you adjust. If you were sleeping with someone who generated a lot of body heat, try turning up your electric blanket. If the spot next to you seems unbearably empty, you might try hugging a pillow or moving over onto his or her side of the bed. You may also find it useful to redecorate the room or simply change the furniture around so that the environment is a little different. Finally, if you are afraid of being alone at night, you may want to bring in a security expert to help burglar-proof your home. Whatever you decide, do remember to make your sleep environment as pleasant and safe as possible.

About Worry

Once you're in bed, you may find yourself so busy thinking and worrying that you can't sleep. Find a way to manage your thoughts. There are several ways to do this.

One way is to externalize these thoughts. Write down all your worries and "things to do" before you turn out the light. Look at the list (which you may find is far less overwhelming than you thought) and decide which things you can control and which things you can't. Plan to deal with the things you can control in the near future. Try to accept that you can't control the others. Then when you put down the paper and pen, give yourself permission to let go of all concerns until tomorrow.

Another strategy is called "thought-stopping." When you find yourself thinking, worrying or tensing up, tell yourself firmly to stop. Then try one of the following tactics:

1. Replace your thoughts with a relaxing fantasy – walking on a beach, floating through clouds, walking in a garden, floating on a raft in the water. Pay attention to the details in your fantasy. Try to see, hear, smell, feel and taste the scene you've created.

2. Focus on your breathing. Count "one" as you breathe in and again as you breathe out. Then count "two" as you breathe in and again as you breathe out. Continue in this manner until you reach "five." After that, go back to "one" again. This strategy helps to clear the mind of the clutter that prevents sleep.

3. Start counting and concentrate on counting as high as you can before a thought interrupts you. When it does, simply return to "one" and start counting again. This allows you to refocus every time you are sidetracked by a distressing thought.

These are some diversionary tactics that can be used to help you sleep. Experiment until you find one that works for you. If these don't work, you may find other suggestions in the books listed in the **Resources** section.

If you still can't sleep . . .

Should you just lie there? The answer to this varies with the individual. If you can lie in bed without worrying about your situation or your insomnia, the rest will do you good even if you aren't sleeping. However, if you are lying in bed agonizing about life or your inability to sleep, you may be better off turning on the light and doing something, even if it's simply reading until you get tired.

Help Yourself to Sleep

If sleep is a problem for you, you may want to work through this assessment.

In the past, rituals that have helped me to sleep include:

_____ going to bed at the same time each night

_____ taking a warm relaxing bath

_____ having a warm drink (caffeine- and alcohol-free)

_____ taking a walk earlier in the evening

_____ listening to relaxing music

_____ reading a light book or magazine

_____ doing relaxation exercises (i.e. meditation or yoga)

_____ making sure the environment is comfortable (paying attention to temperature, lighting, noise)

_____ _____

_____ _____

_____ _____

_____ _____

_____ _____

_____ _____

_____ _____

Things I am doing that may be interfering with my sleep include:

_____ napping during the day

_____ going to bed too early or too late

_____ watching stimulating television (including news) just before bed

_____ reading a challenging book just before bed

_____ drinking beverages with lots of caffeine throughout the day and into the evening

_____ drinking alcoholic beverages in the evening

_____ doing strenuous exercise just before bed

_____ thinking and worrying a lot about problems just before bed

_____ allowing my children to sleep with me

_____ not attending to my sleep environment (too hot or too cold, too light or too dark, too cluttered, uncomfortable pillows or mattress, disturbing noises)

_____ _____

_____ _____

_____ _____

Tonight I will:

_____

_____

_____

Tonight I will not:

_____

_____

_____

Eating Well

Food and Stress

In the period of high stress after the loss of a relationship, some people stop eating well. They eat more (comfort eating) or less or faster than is healthy. Or they choose to eat a lot of fast food and junk food.

Unfortunately, these choices often actually increase the stress the person experiences. Poor eating habits have been linked to mood swings, slower reaction time and an inability to concentrate, as well as lowered resistance to illness. By contrast, eating balanced, regular meals is an excellent way to reduce stress. Healthy eating contributes to a sense of physical and emotional well-being. And it helps to prevent stress-related illnesses.

Healthy Eating: How You Eat

Creating a pleasant environment can aid digestion. Try taking the time to set an attractive table, sit down and focus on the experience of eating. Soft lighting and relaxing music may also add to the experience.

Healthy Eating: What You Eat

A healthy diet is a well-balanced one which does not include the excessive "empty" calories found in alcohol or foods with lots of sugar. It is low in fat, high in fibre and includes selections from each of the following food groups:

- **Protein** – meat, poultry, fish, seafood, cheese, eggs, tofu, peanut butter, etc.
- **Starch** – bread, rolls, crackers, pasta, rice, potatoes, corn, etc.
- **Fruits and vegetables** – apples, oranges, grapes, cantaloupe, beets, carrots, peas, tomatoes, turnips, etc.
- **Fats and oils** – butter, margarine, mayonnaise, cream, salad dressing, nuts, bacon, etc.
- **Milk products** – milk, cheese, yogurt, etc.

A healthy diet also involves eating regularly – at least three complete meals a day (including a good breakfast) or several smaller ones.

There are a wide variety of diets available today. Some are healthy; others are downright dangerous. Unlike many of the fad diets in circulation, the diets designed by the national Diabetes Association and the Weight Watchers organization are particularly healthy and well-balanced. Although they were designed for people who are diabetic and/or dieting, they can be adapted by anyone who wishes to eat well. The diets may include more fruits, vegetables and starches than you are used to and will probably include less meat and fat than you normally eat. You can find out more about these diets by buying one of their cookbooks or by calling or writing to the nearest Weight Watchers Centre or the nearest office of the national Diabetes Association.

If you would like to make some changes to your diet, another option is to work with a nutritionist. Your doctor or local hospital can probably put you in touch with a qualified nutritionist in the area. The nutritionist will talk with you to determine a diet that suits your individual needs and normally schedules several follow-up visits to monitor your progress.

Charting your Food Intake

Use the chart on the following page to keep track of what you consume over a three-day period. Record what you eat and drink (at and between meals) during the three time segments outlined.

Then answer the questions that follow, based on daily consumption. If you answer "No" to several of the questions, you may wish to consult with a dietary specialist or read one of the books suggested in the **Resources** section.

DAY ONE	DAY TWO	DAY THREE
Morning (rising to lunch)	**Morning** (rising to lunch)	**Morning** (rising to lunch)
Afternoon (lunch to dinner)	**Afternoon** (lunch to dinner)	**Afternoon** (lunch to dinner)
Evening (dinner to bedtime)	**Evening** (dinner to bedtime)	**Evening** (dinner to bedtime)

Are You Eating Well?

1. Do I have at least two servings of milk or milk products (three to four if I am pregnant or breast feeding) every day?

   Yes _____   No _____

2. Do I have at least two servings of meat, fish, poultry or other protein every day?

   Yes _____   No _____

3. Do I have at least three to five servings of bread or cereals every day?

   Yes _____   No _____

4. Do I have at least four to five servings of fruits and vegetables every day?

   Yes _____   No _____

5. Have I limited the amount of fat I consume every day?

   Yes _____   No _____

6. Do I drink at least eight glasses of water every day?

   Yes _____   No _____

7. While consuming some alcohol seems to contribute to a healthy heart, excessive alcohol consumption is not healthy. Am I drinking appropriate amounts of alcohol (less than three ounces) per day?

   Yes _____   No _____

8. Excessive caffeine consumption is unhealthy and can contribute to stress. Am I consuming appropriate amounts of caffeine (found in chocolate bars, coffee, tea and cocoa)?

   Yes _____   No _____

9. Am I controlling the amount of "empty calories" I consume in the form of sweets and alcohol?

   Yes _____   No _____

10. Am I consuming 30 grams (1 oz.) of dietary fibre per day?

    Yes _____   No _____

Exercise

Dealing with loss frequently results in depression and fatigue. This may make the prospect of physical exercise seem more trouble than it's worth. However, engaging in physical activity right now is particularly useful for a number of reasons.

Why Exercise?

One of the most important reasons to exercise on a regular basis is that physical exercise increases the blood supply to your brain. As the amount of oxygen that reaches your brain increases, you are apt to feel less tired and more able to concentrate. Thinking clearly is especially important during times of stress.

Increasing physical activity also helps you relax and cope with stress more effectively. Exercising gives you more energy with which to manage your life. Moreover, some of the chemicals released in the brain during exercise are natural mood elevators. They improve your state of mind so that you feel better able to deal with your situation.

You will also improve your general physical health by exercising regularly. Your cardiovascular (heart) fitness is improved so that you are less likely to experience heart problems, including high blood pressure. You may also sleep better and lose weight – both of which contribute to your overall physical health.

How to Get Started

Once you have decided to increase your level of physical activity, you must overcome the hurdle of inertia. Getting started is often the hardest part.

Set reasonable goals. If you are out of shape, start by promising yourself that you will engage in some kind of physical exercise for at least five minutes each day. (For example, walking at a fast pace around the block while swinging your arms as if you mean business.) Then, when you are comfortable with that level of activity, simply increase it.

It takes about three weeks for something to become part of your routine – a habit. So for at least three weeks, be ruthless with yourself. Make yourself engage in physical activity whether you're "in the mood" or not. Then reward yourself afterwards (although preferably not with a huge hot fudge sundae!). After you have begun to be successful, you will find it a lot easier to continue.

When and How Much?

Experts generally agree that in order to stay physically fit, you should exercise moderately for twenty to thirty minutes at least three times a week. By "moderately" they mean exercising hard enough to raise your heart rate, but not so hard that you are out of breath. You should be able to have a conversation with someone while exercising. If you find that exercise increases your sense of emotional well-being, there is no reason to limit yourself to three times a week. A brisk forty minute walk each day, for example, will probably do a world of good. One warning, though: some people don't like to do the same thing every day. After a while they give up their exercise program because they're bored. If you think this may be the case, try to do something different at least once or twice a week. Walk most days, for example, but ride a bike on the weekend. Or go to aerobics classes three times a week and take a walk on the other days. Also, after the first three weeks, feel free to take a day off now and then.

Remember to listen to your body. If it hurts, stop. A lot of people still believe that old saying about "no pain, no gain." Not true! If there's pain, your body is sending you a message. Respect the message and you'll avoid unnecessary injuries.

Exercising with a Friend

Many people enjoy exercising with a friend. This can be an extremely helpful way to get started on an exercise program or to continue on those days when you're just not motivated.

One of the benefits of exercise is that it can provide temporary relief from your problems. So if you do exercise with a friend, consider carefully whether to avoid discussing emotionally difficult subjects. You may even decide not to talk at all and simply exercise together in companionable silence. The decision is yours.

Doing Something About the Exercise Dilemma

If you have not been setting exercise goals on a weekly basis or if you don't think you're getting enough exercise, try the following assessment.

First, analyze your present level of physical activity:

Day	Minutes	Activity: aerobic/other	Comments
Sunday			
Monday			
Tuesday			
Wednesday			
Thursday			
Friday			
Saturday			

Now, set goals for next week. If you did no exercise, decide to do something at least two or three times a week. If you did get some exercise last week, add a reasonable amount to your schedule, remembering that Rome and Arnold Schwarzenegger weren't built in a day. Moderation is the key.

> Note: *To become and then stay physically fit, you should do some form of **moderately** strenuous aerobic exercise (exercise that makes your heart beat faster) for a minimum of twenty to thirty minutes three times a week. Remember to warm up for about five to ten minutes before and cool down for the same amount of time after the aerobic portion of your exercise program. Doing low-intensity stretching exercises can also be helpful in staying flexible, although they don't count toward your total aerobic exercise time.*

Stress-Reduction Techniques

As we have said before, one of the best stress-reduction techniques is living a healthy, balanced life. Exercising regularly, eating and sleeping well and avoiding drugs (including excessive amounts of caffeine and alcohol) are all keys to reducing stress.

Sometimes, however, healthy living isn't quite enough. The exercises described below are designed to help you relax and reduce feelings of stress. They require no special equipment and don't cost a penny. You can do the exercises almost anywhere, although a restful environment free from interruptions is ideal. Wear loose, comfortable clothing if at all possible.

Below, you will find a brief description of each technique. (The techniques are described in more detail in the books found in the **Resources** section.)

Progressive Muscle Relaxation

This technique has been developed to help you relax each set of muscles in your body. The following exercise is probably the simplest of the progressive muscle-relaxation exercises:

Starting at the head or at the feet, tense and then consciously relax each muscle group in order (muscles in the head and face first, then in the neck, then in the shoulders, down to the feet).

For each muscle group, carefully note and appreciate the difference between the feeling of tension and the feeling of warmth and heaviness that results from relaxing the muscles.

Don't rush. The exercise should take about fifteen minutes to complete.

Breathing

You can promote relaxation by focusing in various ways on your breathing. The exercise that follows is simple, but extremely effective: settle into a comfortable position (many prefer to be lying down) and begin deep, abdominal breathing. You can check your breathing by putting one hand on your abdomen, the other on your chest. When you inhale, your abdomen should rise more than your chest does. Now pay close attention to your breathing; try to breathe deeply with each individual inhalation and exhalation. This exercise is beneficial because it forces you to breathe deeply (something we often don't do when under stress) and encourages relaxation.

Meditation

Meditation is an attempt to focus your attention on one thing and close out the rest of the world. The most common type is "mantra meditation." First, get in a comfortable position and take several deep breaths. Then select a mantra (a word or syllable such as "om") and chant it. If a thought interferes, note the thought and then gently dismiss it, returning your attention to your mantra. When you begin, you may only be able to concentrate for a short period of time. With practice, however, you should be able to meditate for longer. Experts suggest that twenty to thirty minutes of meditation once or twice a day will help you reduce stress significantly.

Visualization

Visualization is the technique of using your imagination to create a scene in your mind that is comforting and relaxing. Find a comfortable position and relax all of your muscles. Now create an image in your mind's eye that you find calming and relaxing. For example, imagine floating in a sea of puffy clouds or lying on a warm beach. Or you might want to visualize all the tension seeping out of you like sand flowing out of a pail. You can choose any image you want as long as it promotes a feeling of well-being and calm. (It's important that this is a relaxing image. Winning a million dollars might seem like a pleasant thought, but it could very well stimulate rather than relax you!)

Self-Hypnosis

Self-hypnosis is another technique to help relax. It is based on the premise that you can use a relaxed state to focus on making positive changes in your life, that you can suggest to yourself how you want to act, feel or think in the future. Once you have become deeply relaxed (the "hypnotic state"), you repeat a strong positive statement or visualize a positive image. This "autosuggestion" or "post-hypnotic suggestion" can help make a positive change in your life. And the relaxation you experience will enhance your sense of well-being.

With practice, stress-reduction techniques are relatively easy to use. To get the full picture, you will probably need more information than we have space to provide. If these techniques interest you, be sure to consult the **Resources** section.

Self-Talk

Background

Thinking is generally a positive and useful activity. If thoughts are irrational, however, they may contribute to our problems rather than to our solutions.

One of the ways to deal with this problem is a technique called "cognitive restructuring" or changing the way we talk to ourselves about ourselves and about our world.

One of the premises underlying this technique is that events themselves do not affect us. Instead, it is our belief about an event that determines the effect it has on us. Thus, two individuals observing the same incident will likely perceive it differently.

Moreover, our views are formulated early. We learn to interpret the world during our first interactions, which are generally with our families. We believe the things said to us and about us when we are young, and incorporate these beliefs into the way we think about ourselves.

We continue to hold these beliefs as adults, even though they may no longer be appropriate. A child whose cautious mother told her over and over to be careful may, as an adult, be severely hampered by her inner voice repeating messages that prevent her from living fully (e.g. *"Taking risks is dangerous. I must be careful"*).

Self-Talk

One way of dealing with the irrational messages we repeat to ourselves is to modify our self-talk. Self-talk is what we do when we send silent messages to ourselves such as *"I can't stand it if he leaves me."* We often don't pay attention to what the message is really saying which can often be quite irrational. (e.g. *"I will not be able to survive on my own if he leaves me."*)

Through self-talk, we make meaning out of events. If the self-talk is positive and rational (e.g.*"I feel bad about the divorce and can see where we both made mistakes, but I will survive and may even grow as a result of this experience"*), then we see the event in a healthy way. If, on the other hand, our self-talk is negative (e.g. *"The break up is all my fault and the marriage would have succeeded if I had just worked a little harder"*), we may interpret the events in a self-destructive way.

What to Do About Irrational Self-Talk

First, start paying close attention to your self-talk. Find out what you say to yourself about yourself and about the situations you find yourself in. When you discover what you have been saying, start disputing the irrational thoughts. Replace an irrational message with a reality statement. (Replace *"If he leaves me, I'll die"* with *"If he leaves me, I will be very sad for a time but I will eventually get over it and survive."*)

In other words, changing your self-talk involves:

Detecting

When you find yourself with an unwanted thought, concentrate on it. Know clearly that it's in your head. After the loss of your relationship, for example, you might cause yourself great inconvenience and distress by avoiding going anywhere alone. While examining your self-talk, you might discover that you have been telling yourself you'll die if you have to be seen in public alone. (*"If people see me alone, they'll know I've been divorced and I'll die."*) Examine that thought. Be aware that it is determining your actions.

Disputing

Out loud or to yourself, yell "STOP!" Some people find it helpful to use an elastic band around their wrist. When they identify the unwanted thought, they snap the band as they tell themselves to stop so that they can both feel and hear the request.

Next, tell yourself why this thought is irrational or destructive. Dispute it clearly, using evidence if possible. (*"No, I will not die if I am seen alone. And no one will automatically know I've been divorced because I am not wearing a sign on me that says 'I've been divorced.' Lots of people are alone much of the time and no one I know of has ever died from it. I may feel uncomfortable initially, but I certainly won't die.")*

Displacing

Displace the irrational thought with a positive, rational one. (*"By going into that restaurant alone, I will be proving to myself that I am strong."*) This positive message will make it easier for you to overcome your fears.

At this time, you may also want to rehearse what the change will look like. Imagine walking confidently into the restaurant, head held high. Imagine how good it will feel to overcome your fear. As with a theatre production, rehearsal makes the actual performance smoother, easier and less terrifying.

One last thought . . .

You may have some difficulty changing your negative messages into positive ones. That's natural. It took a long time to learn them. Be kind to yourself by making your expectations reasonable.

Assertiveness

Some people have never learned the challenging, yet rewarding, task of acting assertively. Some, during the painful collapse of an important romantic relationship, lose the ability they once had. They feel overwhelmed by the break up or by the loss itself and begin to react in a passive or hostile way. Here then is a reminder of what assertiveness is.

What is Assertiveness?

Assertiveness, at its simplest, is the ability to assert our own rights without violating the rights of others. And while it's relatively easy to define, it takes a lot of practice to become a truly assertive person.

On the other hand, the alternatives are not ideal. We can react passively, allowing others to impose on us so that our rights are violated. In this case, we keep the peace, but at great personal cost. We rarely get our needs or desires met and we're probably storing up a whole lot of anger and resentment. Or we can become aggressive, imposing our rights on others. In this case, we get our needs and desires met, but we hurt other people in the process. And ultimately, people will probably not want to spend time with us. Some people fluctuate between passive and aggressive behavior. This means that, added to the usual problems associated with these behaviors, these people perceive themselves and are perceived by others as inconsistent. They and their friends may never know what reaction to expect, which can be both frustrating and painful.

A great deal has been written about assertiveness, but it's sometimes confusing to try to figure out how a person can learn the skill. Some people use a system called the "LADDER" script to help them. This is a technique that can be used to ask for what you want in a reasonable, assertive manner. On the following page is an example of how a "LADDER" script works:

L **Look** at your rights, as well as what you want and need. Establishing your goal will help you focus.
(e.g.) *I want my ex to stop calling me every night. We've agreed to a divorce, so it's reasonable for me to expect this.*

A **Arrange** the time and place for discussing the problem situation.
(e.g.) *When she calls tonight, I'll ask her if we can meet in the park tomorrow after work to talk.*

D **Define** the problem. Be as specific possible. As a result, you will be able to tell the person which exact behaviors you would like changed. This will also help you avoid bringing up other feelings and information that confuse the issue and make resolution less likely.
(e.g.) *"When you call me at 7:30 every night to tell me how angry and upset you feel, I spend the rest of the evening trying to calm down."*

D **Describe** your feelings. Use "I" messages in your description.
(e.g.) *"I feel confused and upset when you call and then I feel angry for the rest of the evening."*

E **Express** the request firmly and simply.
(e.g.) *"I would like you to stop phoning me every night."*

R **Reinforce** what you want.
(e.g.) *"If you continue to phone every evening, I will start hanging up. This will mean that all our divorce negotiations will have to go through our lawyers which will add to the expense. If you only call me when we need to talk about the divorce, we can save ourselves money and emotional distress."*

Assertiveness takes practice. By using the "LADDER" script, you can begin to deal with people in a more assertive manner. Here are a few other hints that may be helpful when making assertive requests:

1. Practice your script in your mind or with someone else. The more you rehearse, the more prepared you will feel when you confront the person.

2. Body language says a lot about how we feel. When confronting the person, keep your posture erect and confident,

while using appropriate gestures and facial expressions to emphasize your points.

3. Your voice can tell your listener a lot. A kind tone is important, but speak firmly and clearly as well. Your voice should be confident, not apologetic. (Practice will be of great help with this.)

4. Remind yourself often that you deserve what you are requesting. If you feel you are justified, you will be more convincing.

How Assertive are You?

This assessment is based on the assumption that you are a good authority on yourself. It assumes that you have the unquestionable right to your own thoughts, feelings, wants and behaviors. (And, by the way, with those rights go responsibilities!)

Belief	Often	Some-times	Rarely	Never
1. I believe it's okay to put my needs before others' needs.				
2. I am forgiving of myself when I make mistakes.				
3. My feelings are neither right nor wrong; they simply are. I believe I have a right to experience my feelings whatever they may be.				
4. I believe my opinions and convictions are valid.				
5. I believe I have the right to change my mind.				
6. I believe I have the right to fair treatment and the right to protest unfair treatment.				
7. I believe I have the right to interrupt to ask questions when I don't understand.				
8. I believe I have the right to ask for what I need – including help or emotional support.				

Belief	Often	Some-times	Rarely	Never
9. I believe I have the right to feel and express my pain and distress.				
10. I believe I have the right to choose not to follow others' advice.				
11. I believe I have the right to tell others about my value as a human being.				
12. I believe I have the right to recognition for my success and achievements.				
13. I believe I have the right to say "no."				
14. I believe I have the right to be alone – even if others would like to be with me.				
15. I believe I do not have to justify my thoughts, feelings or actions to others.				
16. I believe each individual is responsible for his or her own self and I can only take responsibility for myself.				
17. If others have needs or wishes, I believe they should express them to me directly.				
18. I believe I have the right to please myself and don't always have to worry about pleasing others.				
19. I believe I can choose not to respond to a situation.				
20. I believe I have the right to express my position and try to negotiate any difference.				

If you checked off more "rarely" and "never" answers, you may profit from learning to become more assertive.

This assessment was adapted from "Your Legitimate Rights" as outlined by Davis, Eshelman and McKay in *The Relaxation and Stress Reduction Workbook* (see the **Resources** section).

Loss and Self-Esteem

Self-esteem affects how we deal with any problem, including the loss of a relationship. As you deal with your present situation, you may want to examine your own sense of self and work to enhance it. If so, here are some guidelines.

Definitions

Self-esteem is the conclusion we draw when we evaluate ourselves. When we examine who and what we are, we make judgments that may be positive or negative or, more probably, both. Our self-esteem reflects these judgments.

It's important to remember that self-esteem fluctuates dramatically depending on what is going on in your life. Sometimes you will feel better about yourself, sometimes worse. And although it may not always feel like it, you probably have a lot more control over how you feel about yourself than you think.

Internal Factors Affecting Self-Esteem: What You Think

When we look for ways to boost our self-esteem, we often look everywhere but inside, where self-esteem is rooted. In fact, most of our self-esteem is based on what *we* think, not on what others think.

Much of what you think about yourself now is based on what you learned early in life. And because many teachers and parents teach by pointing out errors, you may have internalized some fairly negative messages. To boost your self-esteem, you need to replace negative messages with positive ones. This takes effort, but is ultimately worthwhile. Refer to the information on self-talk (see page 42) for specific suggestions on how to change your internal messages.

What you want to do is to send yourself more reasonable and positive messages. You probably say some pretty hurtful things to yourself – we all do – but you can change that if you wish. For example, if you get angry and scream at a friend, you may make it into a catastrophe by saying to yourself, "I have just proved that I am a wicked and angry person and my friend will hate me forever." If you put the action in context, though, you will see that (1) your friend will probably forgive you if you ask and (2) getting angry like that once in a while does not make you a wicked person. Your internal message could therefore probably say something like, "It's unfortunate that I got angry like that, but I did. I will find some way to express my regret, ask for forgiveness, and then we can put it behind us."

Internal Factors Affecting Self-Esteem: What You Do

What you do also affects your self-esteem. Many people fear that failure will adversely affect their sense of self and therefore go to great lengths to avoid it. The best way of avoiding failure appears to be to do less. Certainly people who do more have more failures. But interestingly, people who do more also have more successes. And they learn to live with and learn from failure. In order to enhance your self-esteem, it's normally better to do more, not less.

External Factors Affecting Self-Esteem

What others say about you and how they treat you will certainly affect your sense of self. (And in fact many of us accept the judgments of others quite uncritically.) Unfortunately, you can find yourself influenced by someone who causes your self-esteem to plummet.

What can you do? First, recognize that you probably have more control than you think. You can choose to accept what that person says – or not. You can choose to be treated like that – or not. You can choose to ask that person to change – or not. If he or she doesn't change, you can choose to continue your relationship with that person – or not.

The point is that you can set up an environment to enhance self-esteem.

1. Assess your dealings with acquaintances to determine who makes you feel good about yourself. Choose to spend more time with those who do, less time with those who don't.

2. Ask friends and loved ones clearly and directly for what you need to make you feel good about yourself. ("Please tell me what you like about this meal I've made.") Other people may not know what you need because they base their actions on their own needs – which may be very different from yours. ("Oh. I never care what people think about my cooking but if it's important to you, then I'll be happy to tell you what I like . . .") It's therefore entirely reasonable to make sure they understand what you need by making a request.

3. And finally, scan your environment for positives rather than negatives. Be on the lookout for confirmations of what you've done right, rather than for evidence of what you've done wrong. In a group of smiling faces and one disapproving frown, for example, focus on the smiles.

How's Your Self-Esteem?

Here is a simple exercise that we have adapted from *Celebrate Yourself* by Dorothy Corkhill-Briggs. It is designed to give a direct, personal check on your degree of self-esteem. Read the instructions, then close your eyes and follow them.

Sit in a comfortable position, legs and arms uncrossed. Imagine an empty chair facing you. Picture a person who is very special to you sitting on this chair. There may be many such people in your life, but choose only one. It can be any person, alive or dead.

Imagine that person as vividly as you can. See him or her in clear detail: features, clothes, coloring, characteristics. Avoid continuing the exercise until you have this person sharply in focus. Begin to share with this person all the things you admire and respect about him or her. Spell out these thoughts and feelings in such detail that the other would not have the slightest doubt about them. Take as much time as you need to get the message across. Then, bid him or her a gentle goodbye for the time being and open your eyes.

The second half of this exercise again involves closing your eyes after reading the instructions. Once again, be sure you are sitting in a comfortable, open position.

Imagine that you are suddenly twins. (If you are a twin, imagine that you have a new twin who is really you.) Place the other imaginary you on the chair. Take time to see each of your features clearly; note your coloring, clothes and particular characteristics.

Once you have yourself on the chair in vivid detail, tell yourself all the things that you admire about yourself, leaving no detail out. Use this time to focus on the positive aspects. Then reach out and explain how much you respect and like yourself. When you have finished, slowly open your eyes.

You may have found many positive things to say about the other person, but very little about yourself. Or you may have found that as soon as you shared some positive feelings about yourself, you began to think of all your shortcomings. Or you may have discovered that your dialogue about yourself involved only a trickle of positives – nothing very deep. Finally, you may have found that you could speak as wholeheartedly of your admiration for yourself as for the other person.

If you experienced the last situation, you probably have reasonably high self-esteem. If you were unable to be as positive about yourself, continued effort is necessary to be a good friend to yourself.

Aloneness

Losing a partner usually means spending more time alone. And aloneness is often equated with loneliness. There is no doubt that feelings of loneliness are a difficult part of the grieving process. After a time, though, these feelings can be transformed into something more positive, into an opportunity to become more comfortable with ourselves.

Why is Aloneness So Scary?

The answer to this question is linked to the attitudes and beliefs we grew up with and came to call our own. Often the answer is different for men than for women.

Although our society is changing, many women are taught from an early age that they can only be safe and completely fulfilled when they have a man in their life to protect them and give their life meaning. Being alone, then, means being a half, instead of a whole.

Men find being alone difficult for different reasons. They were often raised to expect that women would look after them. And although many men are taking on more of the responsibility, women are still the primary caretakers in most relationships. Furthermore, men's friendships are often different than women's. Men tend to do things together, while women are more likely to talk together. At this extremely difficult time of loss, men may not have a social system that meets their emotional needs. As a result, being alone for a man may feel overwhelming because he is no longer being looked after and because he has a lot of unmet needs for closeness with others.

How to Make Aloneness More Positive

Being alone is not necessarily a bad thing. People in unhappy relationships can be very lonely, while people who have chosen to live on their own are often among the most contented. It's only when being alone is equated with loneliness and failure that it becomes a negative.

Feeling good about being alone involves changing some of your perceptions. Living as a single person becomes an opportunity to learn more about yourself and to build your life around more of your own needs, desires and interests. One way to do this is to work through the exercises in Part Two of this book. As you set goals and write about your experiences, you will be learning about yourself and your needs.

Learning to live alone is as challenging as learning to be in a relationship. Both take work. An important component of making aloneness work *for* you is to work *at* it. You must find out what you need to do in order to create a new lifestyle for yourself that allows you to enjoy being alone. And then you must do it!

Finally, you will get more out of being on your own if you like who you are and what you do. Once you find ways to become comfortable with yourself and enjoy what you do, you will be in a better position to appreciate life alone and make good decisions about what you want to do with your future.

Attending to Your Social Network

When a romantic relationship dissolves, other important relationships often suffer. Some people respond to loss by avoiding everyone, including the friends who might be best able to help them. The emotional upheaval you experience may also cause you to focus inward - which can put a strain on your friendships. And mutual friends may be difficult to deal with because their loyalties are torn between you and your partner.

Sustaining other relationships can be difficult in times of loss. After all, looking after yourself is tough enough without the added burden of maintaining a friendship. Yet attention to these relationships is particularly important at this time. Friends can provide you with love, support, guidance, even distraction from unhappiness.

As a result, it's important to make the time and find the energy to nourish friendships. Keeping your friendships in good repair is a healthy thing to do.

What Can You Do?

Try to share the talk time. You are probably feeling self-involved right now, which can lead you to monopolize conversations – rehashing your grief, anger, sense of loss. Friends can help you through this time, but it's important to be there for them, too. Ask questions about their lives. Try to listen and respond to concerns, even if they don't seem as important as what's going on in your life. After all, a good friendship involves give and take.

If you are unable to be there for your friends because your own distress is so great, at least share that concern with them. Ask them for feedback about your relationship. Tell them you know the friendship is revolving around you and although you hope to make changes, you are finding it difficult to focus on much beyond yourself at this time. Promise to be there for them as soon as you can. If your friends know you are aware of the situation and are trying to change, they may be more patient and understanding. A good friendship can accommodate a short-term imbalance if the mutual sharing and support are more or less equal over the long term.

Build friendships around more than just talk. Mutual activities like exercising or cooking together, going to a movie or a sports event, can take the focus away from problems. These activities can distract you from your grief and allow you to share some fun with your friends.

Make the effort to initiate contact with your friends. Often they will take responsibility for making contact with you and arranging to see you during the early stages of your grief. Remember to change that pattern as soon as you are feeling a little better so they know you value their friendship.

Try to understand the distress of people who were friends with both you and your partner. It may be tempting to ask these friends to choose between the two of you. But they are probably already experiencing torn loyalties. In fact, you can make their lives easier if you let them know that you don't expect them to choose, that you understand and accept their dilemma.

Finally, if you are unable to move beyond your grief or if your friends seem to be getting impatient, consider seeking professional assistance. Talking with friends can help you work through a difficult time, but sometimes you need more than friends can give. In such cases, you may have to find a way to get your needs met so that your friendships can continue to grow and flourish.

Extending Your Social Network

Often we believe we can meet our social needs within our families (including close romantic relationships) and our careers. People with involving careers and/or complex family demands may decide they don't have time for many friends.

On the other hand, after the loss you have experienced, you may want to extend your social network. When the romantic relationship is gone, children and/or career may not seem like enough.

If you decide to extend your social network, it's important to look for friends, not just potential romantic partners. In fact, if the loss is fairly recent, you would probably be better off avoiding romance completely and focusing instead on finding a few good friends.

Try to include members of both sexes in your new friendships. It's tempting to dump all members of the opposite sex into one category. (*"I've learned my lesson. All men are . . ."* or *"Now I know. All women are . .. ."*) Avoid generalizing. A good friend of the opposite sex can help the healing process.

How Do We Extend Our Social Network?

First, look for new friends in old places – at work, at church, at your child's swimming lesson, through people you already know.

Join something that involves a structured activity. It's sometimes easier to make friends while doing something, even if it's just stuffing envelopes for your favorite charity.

Get involved in something social that has always interested you (say, an environmental group or a theatre group). This will put you in contact with people with similar interests who may become friends.

Try a new activity. This may feel scary, but it also puts you in contact with a number of potential friends. Join an adult swim class and finally learn how to swim. Take that pottery class you always thought you would enjoy. Volunteer to organize an activity for your child's school.

No matter what you decide to do, be sure to enjoy it for its own sake. The object should be to do something different and meet some new people, not to immediately find several best friends. In the long run, you may find a friend or two. In the meantime, you will have become involved in a positive and rewarding experience.

Premature Romantic Involvement

Being on your own after a relationship has ended *is* painful. Even if the relationship was destructive and/or unhappy, alone you may feel worse initially. As a result, you may be tempted to become involved immediately with someone else. But it's important to try to resist that temptation.

While premature romantic involvement is a way of fighting the pain of being alone, it can cause problems. Being finished with one relationship before you start another is *essential*. Otherwise you may bring past issues into the present.

Why We Get Involved Prematurely

Premature involvement often occurs when we fear being alone. But what makes aloneness so frightening? Without really examining it, we often pick up on a message that society (and in particular television, films and advertisers) constantly sends – that to be alone is to be inadequate. Perhaps we assume (consciously or unconsciously) we are alone because of some defect in ourselves that led us to being rejected – we are not worthy of love. These are not happy beliefs. If we accept them, the result is often that we move into a new relationship for all the wrong reasons, out of the perceived need to avoid these negatives rather than because we have chosen an individual as our partner.

How to Avoid a Premature Relationship

First of all, examine your attitudes about being alone. Try to accept that it is not all bad. Given time, you will discover that you can survive and eventually even flourish. One way to achieve this is to pretend that your aloneness is going to end in a month and that you will never have the opportunity to be alone again. This may help you to appreciate your current state and make the most of it.

The problems you had in one relationship almost always surface in the next one unless the underlying issues are resolved. If your past relationship was unhappy, examine what you contributed to the unhappiness. Looking at your own part in it will help you figure out how to be healthier the next time. Identify why you acted the way you did (the causes may date back to your childhood) and look at how you might modify your behavior. Even if you think you will never want to be in another romantic relationship, the insights you have gained will probably make your life much happier. If you'd like to explore the effects of past relationships on your present behavior, Friel & Friel's *Adult Children: The Secrets of Dysfunctional Families* or *An Adult Child's Guide to What is "Normal"* (see the **Resources** section) are two books to consider reading.

Also, recognize that a new relationship is more likely to be successful if you have resolved your feelings about your ex-partner's role in the ending of the relationship. Try to forgive him or her, and if forgiveness is impossible, at least try to understand. Giving yourself time is an important part of this process. Time on your own will allow you to understand yourself and your relationships better. Time on your own will allow you the clarity to see your life more objectively. Time on your own allows you to grieve – so that you can heal – so that you can move on.

Sexuality, Intimacy and the Need for Human Contact

The ending of a romantic relationship often means the loss of a partner who at one time met your needs for emotional and physical closeness and intimacy. You and your partner may not have been sexually active or affectionate for some time or you may have had a fulfilling sex life right up to the end of the relationship. Now that you're on your own, you are probably dealing with feelings of loss relating to your sexuality and your need for intimacy.

Often after the ending of a relationship, feelings of depression result in loss of sexual interest. As well, sexual dysfunctions (such as the inability to attain or maintain an erection or the inability to achieve orgasm) sometimes occur. These experiences may compound feelings of insecurity about sexuality. It's important to remember that these problems are usually directly related to grief and are short-lived.

Another common reaction to loss is an increased interest in sex. You may find yourself thinking about sex a great deal – which usually has more to do with the need for affection than the need for sex itself.

Many people also become sexually active as a way of gaining affection, confirming their attractiveness to others and affirming their own sexuality. While all of these needs may be met through sexual involvement with others, premature emotional entanglements tend to add significantly to existing problems. As well, the risk of contracting a sexually-transmitted disease is frighteningly real. (Some people still choose to become sexually active for a variety of reasons. Of course if you do make this choice, it is important to practise sex in a safe and responsible way.)

While "one night stands" may be immediately gratifying, the most rewarding sexual relationships often occur within the context of trust, open communication, mutual respect and caring. A meaningful relationship takes time and energy to develop. You may not be ready for this yet. If so, there are alternatives to sexual involvement with others.

Individuals on their own often find that friends and family can help to meet the need for affection. Non-sexual hugs and other forms of physical touch can be nurturing and healing. For some, being openly affectionate in a non-sexual way will feel natural; others will have to make an effort to give and receive physical affection from friends or family.

Meeting sexual needs through self-stimulation (masturbation) has developed a new respectability over the years. In fact, virtually all men and most women are sexually active on their own. For those who don't have objections to self-stimulation, the advantage is that one's sexual needs can be relieved without risking premature emotional entanglement.

Affirming your sexual attractiveness to others may also be possible in relationships where it is clear that attraction is present, but both individuals agree that the attraction will not be acted on. You may choose to "date," making it clear to your partners that you are not prepared to become involved in a sexual relationship at this time.

Dating itself may sound scary at first. Often those who have been in relationships for a number of years find that they are in unfamiliar territory because rules and roles for dating and sex may have changed. As with anything else, you will become comfortable with time and practice.

Finally, feeling sensual may not necessarily involve sexual behavior. It can be developed and nurtured in other ways. You may want to find symbols of sexuality that affirm and enhance your feelings about yourself. For example, you might choose to wear a piece of clothing or a scent that in some way represents your sexuality.

Other Losses

The end of a relationship involves more than the loss of a person. Dividing up home, pets, cottage, cars and other possessions can be a painful part of the separation process.

You may be surprised at your feelings of sadness or even anger about the loss of your material possessions. "How can I be so materialistic?" you may ask. "How can I be thinking of *things* at a time like this?"

First, it's important to remind yourself that many people become attached to things that have become familiar and comfortable. In a time of turmoil, it's natural to want those familiar things with you. It's all right to mourn their loss.

One way to help deal with these losses is to try to arrange for a fair and equitable division of your possessions. If it's possible to sit down with your ex-partner and come to a reasonable agreement, this will help you to come to terms with your losses.

Some people are so anxious to leave a relationship that they don't take the time to say goodbye to the things they are leaving behind. If it's possible, try to find a way to gain closure by taking one last look at the things you are leaving. Take mental pictures of the house, the cottage, the favorite chair.

Actual pictures may or may not help. When you find yourself missing your house, you might try looking at old photos. If this helps, keep the photos handy. If it simply makes you feel worse about your losses, put the photos away for a while.

One way of adjusting is to replace things after you've mourned their loss. There can be great excitement in buying new things to match your brand new start.

Sometimes your financial situation will not allow for new purchases. If so, then rearrange existing space and the things you do have so that you've created a new space for yourself. Creating an environment that expresses your individuality is an important step in letting go.

Immediate Financial Decisions

The end of a relationship often brings about a change in your financial status. You may be facing a reduced family income. You may be looking at the need to begin to work outside the home. You may be forced to divide assets and sell a home or a business. You may have to refinance a house in order to buy out your ex-partner. In fact, your financial life may be changing dramatically in any number of ways.

To cope with these changes, here are some basic steps you can take:

1. Learn as much as possible about your own financial situation. You may want to begin by listing all of your assets (what you own) and liabilities (what you owe).

2. Tabulate all of your expenses for a one year period. From this figure determine your monthly expenses.

3. Compare your expenses with the income you expect. Ascertain whether your income will meet your expenses and if you have room in your budget for savings.

4. Consult a financial adviser to help you deal with your financial planning, including life insurance and income tax planning. (Although an adviser can be helpful, do take full responsibility for your own finances. Don't give away control of your finances to anyone else. There are excellent books and short courses to help you develop financial expertise.)

5. Begin to keep good financial records. (Your adviser may be able to help you here.)

6. Consult a lawyer about changes that need to be made to custody arrangements and your will.

7. If necessary, establish a credit rating for yourself. To do this, you can begin to apply for credit cards and perhaps even take out a very small loan. (If you receive credit cards, use them responsibly. In particular, avoid using your cards for comfort spending.)

Initially the prospect of managing your finances can be frightening. It may be tempting to make decisions quickly – particularly if your financial situation looks bleak. Go slow if you can. Most decisions can wait at least a month, possibly longer. Gather the information needed in order to make reasoned, rather than impulsive, decisions.

Loss and Your Job

While you are coping with loss, you may sometimes feel that the responsibility of holding down a job is overwhelming. But there are several advantages to having a job at this time.

First, a job provides structure. When you experience change, it's useful to have some order in your life because it keeps you moving forward. The loss of a relationship can mean that much of your personal life is in chaos, and therefore your job may be one of the few things that continues to provide you with the structure you need.

Second, your job provides you with important interpersonal contacts. Depending on the circumstances of your loss, you may also lose contact with some of the people who would normally give you comfort – your ex-partner's family, for example, and people who were primarily his or her friends. If you have a job, your co-workers can provide you with much needed support.

Finally, your job can give you a sense of accomplishment and achievement. The loss of a relationship can negatively affect self-esteem. Competence at work can do much to counteract this loss of confidence.

Dealing with Potential Job Problems

As we have seen, the process of grief can interfere with fulfilling commitments. Emotional fluctuations and difficulties in concentrating and getting motivated may spill over into your workplace, causing performance problems. The result can be a decline in self-esteem which may be further exacerbated if you are reluctant to tell others about your struggles.

What can you do? Here are some strategies you can use to deal with these work-related concerns:

1. Talk with the appropriate person (normally your immediate supervisor) about what is going on. Explain any unusual behavior and ask for support through this difficult time. If you normally give a great deal to your job, in consultation with your supervisor you may be able to lower your expectations of yourself for a while. Simply adjusting these ex-

pectations may decrease the pressure you feel and help you to get back to normal more quickly. Ask about your performance so that you know where you stand. An objective observer will normally affirm that your performance is less affected by your grief than you had thought.

2. Many organizations recognize the fact that personal difficulties affect work and have developed employee assistance programs (EAP's) that may include counselling services, peer support and more. Ask your supervisor or Human Resources Department about what assistance, if any, is available.

3. To deal with emotional fluctuations, disclosure to others sometimes helps. Colleagues are often willing to provide reassurance and comfort. Keep in mind that a relationship with a colleague is like a friendship: balance and mutual support are crucial. You may first want to check that your co-workers are willing to be involved and that you can find an appropriate time to talk.

4. If you are having difficulty concentrating because of your concerns about your situation, set aside a regular "worry time." At lunch or in the evening, use fifteen to thirty minutes to worry and don't stop until your time is up. Then, when you become preoccupied with concerns (at work or elsewhere), tell yourself that you will think about these things during the designated time, and follow through on this intention. Giving yourself permission to think about your troubles later allows you to concentrate on the task at hand. You may soon find that you have trouble filling your "worry time."

5. Getting motivated can be a problem. To deal with this concern, set small manageable goals. If you have to write a report, for example, this task can be subdivided so that it doesn't feel so overwhelming. One goal might be to collect all the materials you need. Your next goal would be to do the background research. Then decide how you will organize it. And so on. Each of these smaller goals seems less overwhelming than the larger task.

6. Building rewards into your goal-setting is also helpful. Rewards don't have to be job-oriented, but they should be attractive to you. When you finish the report, for example, you might give yourself permission to buy something special or to arrange to have dinner with a friend.

7. Finally, if your job is unsatisfying, the loss you have experienced will probably underline your dissatisfaction and you may feel the need to make a career change. If so, consult the section on **Career Goal Setting** in Part Three.

Loss and Children

Dealing with children while you are mourning the loss of a relationship poses special challenges. While children can be helpful and provide comfort, the responsibility for their care and well-being can be difficult and even frightening at a time when you are feeling so fragile.

No matter what the circumstances, children need to do their own grieving and they need to be reassured. You can contribute significantly to their sense of security and their ability to grieve. Here are a few guidelines to help you help your children:

1. Talk to them about what is going on. Explain what has happened and as much as you know about what will happen in the future. Encourage them to ask questions that will help them to understand.

2. Allow them to express their feelings. They should feel free to talk about their sadness, love, anger and fears.

3. Loss reminds children that many things are beyond their control. Help them to feel more in control by offering them choices, when appropriate. Also take the time to point out what they are able to control.

4. Reassure them that they are not to blame, that no matter what the circumstances, they did not cause the situation.

5. Be open about how you are feeling without burdening them with inappropriate information. Children pick up on how you are feeling even if it isn't expressed verbally so "putting on a brave front" can confuse them. Explain that you are unhappy, but reassure them you can cope or are getting help in coping.

6. Continue to enforce family rules. Make sure that your children know there are still firm guidelines governing their behavior. Avoid indulging them in order to try to "make it up to them."

7. Try to summon as much energy as possible for your times with them. This will be difficult if you are depressed, but

low energy can be interpreted as withdrawal or rejection by your children, adding to their sense of loss.

8. If necessary, expand your social network to get the support you need so that you don't rely on them to provide all your support. After all, you're still the parent and they're still the children. (Do, however, continue to include them in some of your social activities.)

9. Don't ask them to choose sides. Of course, most parents wouldn't make this request directly, but they may do so unconsciously in a number of ways. If, for example, you talk a lot about how much you miss them when they're with the other parent, they may interpret your statement as a request to choose. Similarly, if you talk about how you were wronged in the relationship, they may feel confused about where their loyalties should lie and about whether they can be "on your side" and your ex-partner's, too.

10. Recognize that no matter how angry or hurt you may feel, it is generally better for children to be involved in some way with both parents. Reassure them that you believe this.

11. Never use the children in any way to express your anger at your partner.

12. Find them professional help if they are having a great deal of difficulty coping and don't seem to be recovering after a reasonable amount of time has passed.

Assessing Your Child's Experience of Loss

After the initial separation, you may want to assess how your child is dealing with the loss. The following checklist can be used as an indicator of potential problems.

Does your child experience:

_____ Pervasive sadness

_____ Moodiness

_____ Difficulty concentrating

_____ Frequent somatic complaints (physical symptoms such asheadache, stomachache, etc.)

_____ Frequent nightmares

_____ Changes in school performance

Have there been changes in behavior such as:

_____ Increased aggressiveness (temper tantrums, hitting)

_____ Clinging

_____ Frequent crying spells

_____ Unusual restlessness

_____ Difficulty sleeping

_____ Regressing to an earlier stage of development (such asbedwetting in a toilet-trained child)

_____ Inability or lack of desire to play

_____ Compulsive overeating or loss of appetite

If your child is displaying two or more of these symptoms, you may want to contact your doctor or a mental health specialist to discuss how you can help your child adjust to the family's loss.

Relationships with Your "Ex" and His or Her Family

When a relationship ends, it may be necessary to continue to see your ex-partner and his or her family on a regular basis. If you have children, live in a small town or work in the same office, for example, you will be thrown into contact more often than may be comfortable.

The Relationship with Your Ex-Partner

Some people wish to "remain good friends" with their ex-partners, particularly if they made the decision to leave the relationship. Being friends rarely happens without concerted effort from both parties. And often the best that is possible is a relationship that's amiable but not close.

Other people are so angry that they never want to see their ex-partner again. Some continue to play out their anger and hurt by using their children as instruments to inflict pain. Unfortunately, the children suffer most in this scenario as they are forced to choose sides, to choose between the two people they love most in the world.

If you must interact regularly, it is important to establish a civil relationship with your ex-partner. This may be difficult because civility seems to imply forgiving him or her for wrongs committed during your time together. But you can be amiable even if it feels impossible to entirely forgive. As you establish this new relationship and begin to accept responsibility for some of the problems that occurred, many of your negative feelings will probably subside.

A distant, but pleasant, relationship between parents where there is no expressed anger, hostility and resentment is much easier for children to handle. Warmth is not necessary if it is impossible for you, but the absence of malice will make the situation better for all concerned.

The Relationship with Your Ex-Partner's Family

If you have been in a relationship for a long time, your ex-partner's extended family may have become part of your social network. The loss of your partner will probably seriously affect your relationship with his or her family.

Sometimes families believe they must choose sides. They may close ranks around their family member and exclude you – even if there had been warm and friendly interactions before. If this is happening, you may wish to contact your ex-partner's family (by telephone or letter or in person) to express your sadness about losing them and your wish to continue a relationship – for yourself or, if there are children, for their sake. If they are able, the family will respond positively. If they are not, you may have to let it go for the moment.

The new relationship you build with his or her family will doubtless have its awkward moments. When these moments occur, try to deal with them without overreacting. Humor can help. So can distancing yourself. You can choose to let things go. Try being an observer, rather than a participant, in the situation. By pulling back emotionally, you can minimize the impact of interactions that would normally distress you.

Perhaps most importantly, give the family the benefit of the doubt. People often create awkward moments through thoughtlessness, rather than malice. If your ex-sister-in-law calls you by the name of his new wife, try assuming that this was because of confusion, rather than a desire to hurt you. And let it go.

If it helps, remember that you are not alone. Many relationships break up and society is becoming more accepting and less judgmental of the individuals involved. More and more families are dealing with the reality of multiple relationships and as a result it may become easier (although never easy!) to incorporate previous as well as current members into the extended family.

The Unexpected Reaction

At certain times feelings of grief and loss will be rekindled. These times might include anniversaries of special days that mark the beginning or the end of your relationship, your ex-partner's birthday, the day you moved into your first home together, or your children's birthdays. On these days, your memories may call forth unusually strong feelings of loss.

These unexpected reactions are common among people who have experienced loss. Rest assured that as the day passes, your feelings of sadness will usually pass, too. If you can anticipate these dates, you will be in a better position to handle your reaction. Strategies for dealing with your pain might include writing in your journal, arranging to spend the day with a close friend, renting a movie you want to see or reading a favorite book.

Coping with Holidays

Holidays like Christmas and Thanksgiving are occasions for people to get together. Holidays are times when traditions are particularly important and most of us have strong memories of holidays past. Sometimes these memories are exaggerated—we remember how they should have been, not how they were. Finding yourself alone at holiday time and being nostalgic for times past can feel intolerable. To cope, be prepared to look realistically at yourself and your situation and plan ahead.

Expectations

Most people expect far too much from the holidays. They believe that the family will be in perfect accord; and even at the best of times this doesn't always happen. Try to be realistic about what you expect for the coming holiday. Don't anticipate that people will all get along just because it's the season of goodwill to all men or that you won't be sad simply because 'tis the season to be jolly.

Creating Your Own Traditions

Now that you are alone, you should plan a new approach to the holiday by doing things that hold special meaning for you. Jane Seskin, in *Alone Not Lonely*, suggests making a list of all the things you didn't like about past holidays and another list of all the good things. Throw away the list of bad things and incorporate the good things into your plan. This way you have the opportunity to create a holiday that belongs to you.

Planning Ahead

The best way to avoid holiday disappointments is to plan ahead. Decide well in advance what you want to do and who you would like to do it with. Decide whether you want to be at home or away from home. Do you want to fill your time with activity or would you prefer to have time to think and reflect? Would you like to be with close family members, friends or a combination of the two?

Then make sure you ask those people if they are willing to be a part of your holiday plans. Make the necessary reservations and purchases. Have a "plan B" if your first choice isn't possible.

Dealing with Feelings of Loss

Even with the best of plans and the best of friends, you may find that your feelings of sadness persist. Rather than trying to suppress these feelings, you may want to share them with your companions. Sometimes this will be enough. If not, you have a couple of choices. You can leave for a time to collect yourself. Or you could use the thought-stopping techniques described on pages 42 to 44.

Prolonged Grief Reactions

Feeling sad is a normal part of the grief process. For a while after your loss – perhaps even for a long time – you may experience intense sadness and depression. There is no magic formula that determines how long grief should take or how bad it will feel. And the intensity of your grief is not tied to how positive the relationship was. Instead, it is determined by your emotional attachment to the person you lost. Thus, even the end of a bad relationship, if it was a highly emotional one, will produce strong feelings of grief.

The intensity and duration of grief will differ with each individual. However, sometimes a person's grief is more intense or goes on for longer than is healthy. With this type of grief reaction, you continue to feel overwhelmed by the loss long after you might be expected to be feeling better. You are "stuck" in your grief and are not moving toward resolution of your feelings.

Grief Delayed

Sometimes grieving over the loss of your relationship will be delayed because of other concerns. If, for example, you had to attend to a great many logistical details involved with moving, you might not be able to attend to your personal grief right away. In this case, it is important to remember that the process of grief has simply been delayed. You will still need to mourn your relationship at some point in order to resolve your feelings.

Grief Masked

Occasionally, a person will not experience the normal grief reaction, but will instead experience behaviors or symptoms seemingly unrelated to the loss. These might include medical problems (such as chest pains or some other psychosomatic disorder) or aberrant behavior (such as shoplifting). People who experience grief in this way are at least temporarily masking or suppressing their feelings. As with delayed grief, however, it is important to note that the grief must ultimately be confronted and worked through before resolution can occur.

Grief Avoided

Some people are afraid of grief and avoid thinking about the person whom they have lost. This can be caused by guilt – about things done or undone – or by the fear of pain. And sometimes people are afraid to think too deeply about the person they've lost because they fear they'll lose control of themselves and something terrible will happen. As with delayed and masked grief, the only way to deal with the loss is to confront it and experience the pain so you can move on.

How can you tell if your grief is "prolonged"?

Normally, time and work reduce the intensity of grief. After a reasonable length of time has passed, the following situations or feelings may indicate "prolonged" grief:

- You have made no progress toward resolving your grief.
- You experience intense grief as a result of relatively minor triggers (e.g.)driving past a place you once visited together, watching a movie about divorce on television.
- You keep many of your ex-partner's possessions, constantly play "our song," return frequently to places where you spent time together and so on.
- You take on the hobbies, characteristics or activities of the person you lost – not because you really want to, but because it is a way to keep a part of him or her with you.
- You regularly withdraw from friends, family, your job or other important responsibilities.
- You act on self-destructive impulses.
- You experience an increased number of physical problems (e.g.) frequent colds, back pain, stomach disorders, etc.

When to Get Help

Organized or informal support groups are almost always helpful. Sometimes, however, the assistance of a therapist or other professional may also be necessary.

It may be difficult to determine when you need this type of assistance. If any of the four scenarios below fit your situation after what feels like a reasonable length of time, you may want to explore the possibility of seeking professional help:

1. Your life is very disorganized and you are unable to function effectively in the world and/or in your home.
2. You are able to function when others are present, but are unable to function effectively when alone.
3. You believe a reasonable time has passed and you are still feeling "stuck" in the grief process.
4. You recognized yourself in the descriptions of grief listed above.

When Professional Help is What You Need

Reasons for Considering Additional Help

As you work through your grief, you may consider seeking additional help. Some of the reasons might include the following:

- Your level of distress is so overwhelming that you feel helpless and hopeless. You believe that life has no meaning.
- You believe that you are not in control of your life.
- You don't know what you need to do to change or you are not motivated to make the changes that you think may be necessary.
- You want to improve the quality of your life.

Once you've made the decision to seek help, there are a wide variety of options available. Self-help groups such as Parents Without Partners, Alcoholics Anonymous, Alanon, etc. provide support and may be sufficient. However, you may decide that professional help is what you need.

Types of Professional Help

Many individuals advertise themselves as therapists. You will need to make some decisions about the type of professional you are looking for. You might, for example, choose to consult one of the following: minister (pastoral counsellor), psychiatric nurse, psychiatrist, psychologist or social worker. These individuals may work with you on a one-to-one basis and/or recommend that you join a therapy group, depending on your needs and personal preferences.

How to Choose a Professional

Finding a therapist may be confusing. Here are some suggestions:

1. Ask around. Your family doctor can probably suggest names of competent mental health professionals. If your workplace has an employee assistance program or com-

prehensive human resources department, you can also get answers there. Another option is to contact professional associations and ask for the names of individuals in your area who deal with your particular concern.

2. Seeing a mental health professional is more acceptable than it used to be. There is a good chance that you already know someone who's been to therapy. Thus, you may want to ask your trusted friends for ideas about how to make this choice.

3. You can also use the yellow pages. If you choose this route, be sure to call the individuals you've identified to ask them about their qualifications, experience and approaches to therapy. If you are not comfortable with your phone interaction for any reason, you may want to look elsewhere.

Factors to Consider When Making your Choice

Qualifications: Because individuals can advertise themselves as "therapists" with little or no training, most people prefer to choose someone who has the necessary academic qualifications and is licensed by a recognized association or governing body. For more specific information about this topic, consult *Making Therapy Work* by Fredda Bruckner-Gordon, Barbara Kuerer Gangi and Geraldine Urback Wallman.

Individual Qualities: The individual qualities of the therapist you choose are extremely important. Think about the kind of person with whom you can work comfortably. You may want to consider the therapist's sex and age; religious or spiritual orientation; warmth, openness and sense of humor. When you work with this person, the outcome is more likely to be positive if you feel accepted and supported. Therapy is almost never successful if your therapist seems uncaring and judgmental.

Cost: For many of us, cost is an important factor. Some services are more fully covered by health insurance than others. The first step should be to find out which of these services is covered by your insurance plan. If your workplace has an employee assistance program, you may qualify for further coverage.

When talking to the professional, determine rates and ask if he or she considers basing the fee on your level of income and ability to pay. (If you are seeking help from a government agency, this is likely to be the case.) You may also want to ask if it's possible to work out a payment plan that would fit with your budget.

If you are considering working with someone who is in private practice, the fee is likely to be higher. If you are concerned about the cost, you may contact his or her association or licensing board to ask if the charge is reasonable.

Finally . . .

Remember, if you're not satisfied with your first experience, don't be discouraged. It sometimes takes time to find the right person. Try again, rather than giving up.

Making Meaning

Most of us need to derive meaning from the events we experience. When something bad happens, we look for reasons. As you struggle with your feelings of loss, one of the questions you will probably ask is "Why me?"

Often people try to make sense of a bad experience by identifying past transgressions. "If I could just figure out what I did wrong," they say, "then I could figure out why I am being punished." This becomes particularly difficult if they can't think of any sin large enough to warrant the present punishment.

A more positive approach is to try to discover what you can learn from your loss. What insight could be gained from this experience? What changes do you need to make? In what ways are you growing? What do you plan to do differently in the future? Many people move from one broken relationship to the next without learning from the experience. The attempt to understand may help you avoid making the same mistakes next time.

How can you make meaning?

For many, spirituality offers both comfort and a way to understand and learn from loss. Organized religious groups can provide a sense of community, as well as an opportunity to practise one's faith. If being part of a church group does not fit with your beliefs, then informal spiritual reflection and reading may be more helpful.

Another way to make meaning is to visit the philosophy section of a library or a bookstore. Find a book that appeals to you and your world view. Think about how it relates to your experience.

A further possibility is to talk with others – perhaps a philosopher, a minister or any thoughtful, well-read person. There are also organizations which will help you in your search for understanding. Many of them offer short workshops and retreats or ongoing groups to help you recover from your loss. You can find out about these organizations by looking in a local community service directory or by calling your local library.

For many, journal writing provides an opportunity to reflect on their experiences and understand what has happened. This is one of the reasons why Part Two of this book includes a section asking you to write.

Whether writing or reflecting, it may be helpful to try to fit your loss into the larger context. In this way, you can begin to see your present pain as a part of your journey through life, rather than an isolated negative experience. Whatever you choose, the *attempt* to make meaning will be an important part of the healing process.

$\mathcal{P}$art Two: Weekly Activities and Reflections

Part Two: Weekly Activities and Reflections focuses your time and energy in some positive directions. We've included a list of possible activities that will help you develop a healthier body and another list of activities to nourish your soul. Some are more gender-specific, others are not. Add your own activities for body and soul to these lists whenever you think of them. We suggest that starting today and for the next three months, it would be helpful to fill in the **Activities Sheet** at the beginning of each week.

We also suggest that you do some writing – at the end of each week – on the **Reflections Sheets** included in this section. While you are writing, try answering some or all of the following questions:

- Were any activities particularly rewarding?
- Were you able to identify situations during the week in which you liked yourself better?
- Were there times when you would have preferred to behave differently?

Answering these questions may help you to direct your future, determine what you like to do and who you would like to be. This process also helps you get to know yourself better. You may choose to retain what you like about yourself and modify what you don't, thus building self-esteem and confidence.

Because self-exploration is a never-ending process, we would encourage you to continue with the weekly reflection and writing after the three-month period covered in this book. (For more information about this, refer to the **Introduction.**)

Contents

Activities for the Body

- Get a facial. Do it yourself or get it done by a friend or a professional.
- Go for a swim.
- Join a health club or design your own exercise program.
- Buy a cookbook with healthy and delicious recipes.
- Go for a fast walk or a run.
- Stop or cut down on smoking.
- Get a pedicure. Do it yourself or get it done by a friend or a professional.
- Go to an aerobics class.
- Go for a bike ride.
- Give yourself an at-home hair treatment.
- Go snow or water skiing.
- Get a manicure. Do it yourself or get it done by a friend or a professional.
- Go snowshoeing, golfing or horseback riding.
- If you're female, do a breast self-examination. (But wait until your period is over.)
- If you're male, do a testicular self-examination.
- Stop or cut down on drinking.
- Buy an exercise video and start to use it regularly.
- Get your teeth checked and cleaned.
- Join a weight loss group.
- Go for a hike in the woods or a park.
- Get an extra hour of sleep by arranging to go to bed early.
- Resolve to drink more water (at least eight glasses a day).
- Join a volleyball or basketball group.
- Get a massage.
- Stop or cut down on your use of non-prescription drugs.

- Buy a comfortable pair of shoes.
- Buy some herbal tea and start drinking it in the evenings.
- Do ten sit-ups every day.
- Have your blood pressure checked.
- If you're female and over 40, ask your physician about the advisability of having a mammogram.
- Visit a health food store and buy something unusual.
- Get your eyes checked.
- Buy a relaxation tape and listen to it every night before you go to sleep.

Activities for the Soul

- Soak in a bubble bath surrounded by candles.
- Go to a yoga or Tai chi class.
- Buy yourself flowers.
- Rent a movie and make popcorn.
- Volunteer to help in a hospital or seniors' home.
- Buy or borrow an engrossing book and start to read it.
- Resurrect a hobby you used to enjoy (sewing, stamp collecting, woodworking).
- Listen to upbeat music for an evening.
- Make yourself a special dinner. Decorate the table with candles, your best dishes, cloth napkins, the works.
- Join a service club.
- Go to an art gallery or museum.
- Invite someone to go to the movies with you.
- Organize a messy drawer or closet.
- Get a book from the library on a brand new topic you've always wanted to explore.
- Ask a friend over for tea or coffee (decaf!).
- Do a jigsaw puzzle.
- Buy or make a new piece of clothing or accessory.
- Read up on one of the religions of the world.
- Spend an evening planning what you would do with one million dollars.
- Research the local charities and give money to one of them.
- Write a poem.
- Write a long overdue letter.
- Buy a hard-to-kill plant.
- Treat yourself to afternoon tea.

- Start a collection (buttons, lace, boxes, stamps, butterflies).
- Take a picnic to a park and enjoy people-watching.
- Buy a magazine you wouldn't normally buy and read it cover to cover.
- Phone an out-of-town friend you haven't seen for a long time.
- Change your hairstyle, or grow a mustache or beard.
- Make arrangements to spend a weekend out of town.
- Do a challenging crossword.
- Get makeup advice from a friend or store clerk.
- Lock away or give away the favorite record that makes you gloomy.
- Go to church.
- Join a choir.
- Host a theme pot-luck dinner.
- Pick up brochures and plan an adventure holiday (even if you can't afford to take it).
- Buy some sexy lingerie or underwear.
- List all the nice men you've known.
- List all the nice women you've known.
- Learn a new craft/hobby (knitting, golf or whatever).
- Take a practical evening course (know your automobile, beginner's cooking class).
- Get your colors draped.
- Buy a new kind of vegetable at the grocery store and prepare it.
- Buy a piece of clothing in a bright color you rarely wear.
- List all the best qualities of your friends.
- Redo your budget and start saving for something you've always wanted.

- Buy a cardboard or metal filing cabinet and organize all your papers.
- Figure out how to start to forgive yourself for something you feel guilty about.
- Buy a relaxation tape and use it regularly.
- Buy an exotic or interesting hat and wear it.
- Treat yourself to caviar.
- Buy new sheets for your bed.
- Make or buy a kite and fly it with a friend.
- Learn to make a new kind of salad.
- Try a new restaurant.
- Buy (or resurrect) a teddy bear and hug it once a day.
- Borrow a friend's child and treat him/her to a fun day.
- Sponsor a foster child in a Third World country and start writing letters to him/her regularly.
- Clean out a clothes closet and send the clothes to a women's shelter or other worthy organization.
- Plan a dream home – in detail.
- Take up photography or painting.
- Read a children's classic (*Anne of Green Gables, The Velveteen Rabbit, The Wizard of Oz, The Narnia Tales*).
- Choose an author and read everything he/she wrote.
- Play the soundtrack from your favorite musical or movie.
- Make or buy new curtains or pillows for your bedroom.
- Do some of that mending that's been waiting.
- Ask a friend over to make a batch of some kind of food (jam, chocolates, cookies, egg rolls, spaghetti sauce).
- Rearrange the furniture in one of your rooms.
- Buy flowers or a small gift for a supportive friend.
- Plant a tree.
- Repot a plant.
- Start an indoor herb garden.

- Get up early to watch a sunrise.
- Volunteer to work backstage or on stage with an amateur theatre company.
- List all the things you like about women.
- List all the things you like about men.
- Invite a friend to a (basketball, hockey, football) game.
- Bake cookies for a friend or your co-workers.
- Go Christmas shopping – no matter what month it is!
- Put all your loose photos in an album.
- Visit a shut-in.
- Write a thank-you letter to an old friend or your parents.
- Make a list of all the ways you've improved over the past five years.
- Write a limerick.
- Have lunch with a friend.
- Buy or make a potpourri for your underwear drawer – and start calling it your lingerie drawer!
- Get your fortune told.
- Redecorate a room with new paint or wallpaper.
- List all the things you like about yourself.
- Contact a friend you've neglected for too long.
- Make up a new address book or update the old one.
- Ask your parents for help in collecting information about your ancestors.
- Get a pet.
- Start an investment club with a few friends.
- Go to the zoo.
- Buy a new print or hanging for a bare wall.
- Start making Christmas or birthday gifts for family and friends.
- Learn everything you can about a type of music with which you're unfamiliar.

- Identify an annoying habit and decide how to get rid of it.
- Take an interest course (music appreciation, archaeology).
- Begin a journal.
- Plant an outdoor garden.
- Go to a workshop for the newly separated and/or divorced.

SAMPLE
Activities for Week X
(January 7 to 14)

Body

Select two activities from the **Activities for the Body** list on pages 89 to 90. You may want to choose your own activities. If so, that's wonderful . . . go ahead!

1. Go for a fast walk on Tuesday and Thursday after work.
2. Weed out my clothes closet on Wednesday night.

Soul

Select two activities from the **Activities for the Soul** list on pages 91 to 95. You may want to choose your own activities for this category as well. If so, no problem . . . go ahead!

1. Make a list of all my good qualities on Sunday evening.
2. Call the Volunteer Bureau on Monday to ask about volunteering.

Other Important Things To Do:

1. Call Robin about going to the movies Saturday night.
2. Do the laundry on Saturday morning.
3. _____

SAMPLE
Reflections During Week X
(January 7 to 14)

During this week, I have learned:

– How much I like walking. Must do it more often.

– Was really down on Sunday afternoon. Lay down on the couch and slept for two hours. Then had trouble sleeping on Sun. night. Sun. afternoons are tough.

– Did laundry, but not much else at home. Lists help. Should make them.

– I'm okay. List of my good qualities was a real morale booster.

This week I also thought about:

– How am I going to deal with Shawn when he comes to stay next weekend? I know he's my kid, but I feel uncomfortable when he first arrives. Am I an unnatural parent? Must ask my support group.

– Got depressed on Sun. afternoon because I thought about my ex and the good times we had. Later I remembered the time my ex made fun of Mom at the Christmas table. That made me sad but I felt a little better too.

In the future, I will:

– Make more extensive lists of things to do at home.

– Arrange to do something on Sunday afternoon—preferably with someone.

– Talk to the support group about dealing with Shawn.

– Go for a walk at least twice a week.

In the future, I will not:

– Lie down or go to sleep if I'm feeling depressed.

97

Activities for Week 1

(_____to _____)

Body

Select two activities from the **Activities for the Body** list on pages 89 to 90. You may want to choose your own activities.

1. _____

2. _____

Soul

Select two activities from the **Activities for the Soul** list on pages 91 to 95. You may want to choose your own activities for this category as well.

1. _____

2. _____

Other Important Things to Do:

1. _____

2. _____

3. _____

Reflections during Week 1

(_____to _____)

During this week, I have learned:

_____

_____

_____

_____

This week I also thought about:

_____

_____

_____

_____

In the future, I will:

_____

_____

_____

_____

In the future, I will not:

_____

_____

_____

_____

Activities for Week 2

(_____to _____)

Body

Select two activities from the **Activities for the Body** list on pages 89 to 90. You may want to choose your own activities.

1. _____

2. _____

Soul

Select two activities from the **Activities for the Soul** list on pages 91 to 95. You may want to choose your own activities for this category as well.

1. _____

2. _____

Other Important Things to Do:

1. _____

2. _____

3. _____

4. _____

Reflections during Week 2

(_____to _____)

During this week, I have learned:

_____
_____
_____
_____

This week I also thought about:

_____
_____
_____
_____

In the future, I will:

_____
_____
_____
_____

In the future, I will not:

_____
_____
_____
_____

Activities for Week 3

(_____ to _____)

Body

Select two activities from the **Activities for the Body** list on pages 89 to 90. You may want to choose your own activities.

1. _____

2. _____

Soul

Select two activities from the **Activities for the Soul** list on pages 91 to 95. You may want to choose your own activities for this category as well.

1. _____

2. _____

Other Important Things to Do:

1. _____

2. _____

3. _____

4. _____

Reflections during Week 3
(_____ to _____)

During this week, I have learned:

_____
_____
_____
_____

This week I also thought about:

_____
_____
_____
_____

In the future, I will:

_____
_____
_____
_____

In the future, I will not:

_____
_____
_____
_____

Activities for Week 4

(_____to _____)

Body

Select two activities from the **Activities for the Body** list on pages 89 to 90. You may want to choose your own activities.

1. _____

2. _____

Soul

Select two activities from the **Activities for the Soul** list on pages 91 to 95. You may want to choose your own activities for this category as well.

1. _____

2. _____

Other Important Things to Do:

1. _____

2. _____

3. _____

4. _____

Reflections during Week 4

(_____to _____)

During this week, I have learned:

_____
_____
_____
_____

This week I also thought about:

_____
_____
_____
_____

In the future, I will:

_____
_____
_____
_____

In the future, I will not:

_____
_____
_____
_____

Activities for Week 5

(_____to _____)

Body

Select two activities from the **Activities for the Body** list on pages 89 to 90. You may want to choose your own activities.

1. _____

2. _____

Soul

Select two activities from the **Activities for the Soul** list on pages 91 to 95. You may want to choose your own activities for this category as well.

1. _____

2. _____

Other Important Things to Do:

1. _____

2. _____

3. _____

4. _____

Reflections during Week 5

(_____to _____)

During this week, I have learned:

_____
_____
_____
_____

This week I also thought about:

_____
_____
_____
_____

In the future, I will:

_____
_____
_____
_____

In the future, I will not:

_____
_____
_____
_____

Activities for Week 6

(_____to _____)

Body

Select two activities from the **Activities for the Body** list on pages 89 to 90. You may want to choose your own activities.

1. _____

2. _____

Soul

Select two activities from the **Activities for the Soul** list on pages 91 to 95. You may want to choose your own activities for this category as well.

1. _____

2. _____

Other Important Things to Do:

1. _____

2. _____

3. _____

4. _____

Reflections during Week 6

(_____to _____)

During this week, I have learned:

_____

_____

_____

_____

This week I also thought about:

_____

_____

_____

_____

In the future, I will:

_____

_____

_____

_____

In the future, I will not:

_____

_____

_____

_____

Activities for Week 7

(_____ to _____)

Body

Select two activities from the **Activities for the Body** list on pages 89 to 90. You may want to choose your own activities.

1. _____

2. _____

Soul

Select two activities from the **Activities for the Soul** list on pages 91 to 95. You may want to choose your own activities for this category as well.

1. _____

2. _____

Other Important Things to Do:

1. _____

2. _____

3. _____

4. _____

Reflections during Week 7
(_____to _____)

During this week, I have learned:

_____

_____

_____

_____

This week I also thought about:

_____

_____

_____

_____

In the future, I will:

_____

_____

_____

_____

In the future, I will not:

_____

_____

_____

_____

Activities for Week 8
(_____to _____)

Body

Select two activities from the **Activities for the Body** list on pages 89 to 90. You may want to choose your own activities.

1. _____

2. _____

Soul

Select two activities from the **Activities for the Soul** list on pages 91 to 95. You may want to choose your own activities for this category as well.

1. _____

2. _____

Other Important Things to Do:

1. _____

2. _____

3. _____

4. _____

Reflections during Week 8
(_____to _____)

During this week, I have learned:

_____
_____
_____
_____

This week I also thought about:

_____
_____
_____
_____

In the future, I will:

_____
_____
_____
_____

In the future, I will not:

_____
_____
_____
_____

Activities for Week 9

(_____to _____)

Body

Select two activities from the **Activities for the Body** list on pages 89 to 90. You may want to choose your own activities.

1. _____

2. _____

Soul

Select two activities from the **Activities for the Soul** list on pages 91 to 95. You may want to choose your own activities for this category as well.

1. _____

2. _____

Other Important Things to Do:

1. _____

2. _____

3. _____

4. _____

Reflections during Week 9
(_____to _____)

During this week, I have learned:

_____

_____

_____

_____

This week I also thought about:

_____

_____

_____

_____

In the future, I will:

_____

_____

_____

_____

In the future, I will not:

_____

_____

_____

_____

Activities for Week 10

(_____to _____)

Body

Select two activities from the **Activities for the Body** list on pages 89 to 90. You may want to choose your own activities.

1. _____

2. _____

Soul

Select two activities from the **Activities for the Soul** list on pages 91 to 95. You may want to choose your own activities for this category as well.

1. _____

2. _____

Other Important Things to Do:

1. _____

2. _____

3. _____

4. _____

Reflections during Week 10

(_____to _____)

During this week, I have learned:

_____

_____

_____

_____

This week I also thought about:

_____

_____

_____

_____

In the future, I will:

_____

_____

_____

_____

In the future, I will not:

_____

_____

_____

_____

Activities for Week 11
(_____to _____)

Body

Select two activities from the **Activities for the Body** list on pages 89 to 90. You may want to choose your own activities.

1. _____

2. _____

Soul

Select two activities from the **Activities for the Soul** list on pages 91 to 95. You may want to choose your own activities for this category as well.

1. _____

2. _____

Other Important Things to Do:

1. _____

2 _____

3. _____

4. _____

Reflections during Week 11
(_____to _____)

During this week, I have learned:

_____

_____

_____

_____

This week I also thought about:

_____

_____

_____

_____

In the future, I will:

_____

_____

_____

_____

In the future, I will not:

_____

_____

_____

_____

Activities for Week 12

(_____to _____)

Body

Select two activities from the **Activities for the Body** list on pages 89 to 90. You may want to choose your own activities.

1. _____

2. _____

Soul

Select two activities from the **Activities for the Soul** list on pages 91 to 95. You may want to choose your own activities for this category as well.

1. _____

2. _____

Other Important Things to Do:

1. _____

2. _____

3. _____

4. _____

Reflections during Week 12

(_____to _____)

During this week, I have learned:

_____

_____

_____

_____

This week I also thought about:

_____

_____

_____

_____

In the future, I will:

_____

_____

_____

_____

In the future, I will not:

_____

_____

_____

_____

$\mathcal{P}$art Three: Putting it All Together

Part Three: Putting it All Together is designed to help you set some long-term goals, to seriously examine your plans for the future. Most people need some time to grieve before they are able to focus on setting goals. You may want to save part or all of this section until a time when you are feeling prepared to look positively and even hopefully at your future.

Contents

Setting Goals

Most of us want to "live happily ever after." Normally we associate this phrase with fairy tales. The knight in shining armor rescues the helpless heroine. The poor woodsman is rescued from a life of drudgery by the beautiful princess who wants him for her own.

Welcome to the real world! Fortunately, in this world, we are not helpless; we don't need someone else to rescue us; we can make the happy ending come about all on our own.

In the next few pages, you'll be setting goals for yourself, goals that will give you the power to make your life better, happier, more meaningful, or whatever it is that you want.

What are Goals?

Goals are directions for action. Before you set goals, you assess your life now and decide where you want to be. You can (and will!) make goals for many aspects of your life. And the more specific you get, the more likely you are to reach those goals.

Why Set Goals?

Why, indeed. Perhaps the simplest explanation is this: if you don't know where you're going, how will you know when you get there?

But beyond that, setting goals helps you to move forward on a path that makes sense. You can certainly get to interesting places without setting goals. But especially in times of distress, it's helpful to have something to work for, something that makes you feel like you're moving ahead.

How Do I Set Goals?

Setting goals involves reflection – on the past, the present and what you want for the future.

First, look at who you are. What are your talents, abilities, skills, enthusiasms? By assessing these, your thoughts begin moving in the right direction.

Then start dreaming. Look into the future and let your imagination take you to exciting new places. (Kids do it all the time. It's called "daydreaming" and it's fun.) Remember, if you focus too much on reality at first, you may cut yourself off from some important possibilities. So dream first. Brainstorm. Don't evaluate. Just let the ideas flow – and write them all down.

After you've generated an exciting list of possibilities, you may need to get more information about some of them. Figure out where you can get what you need – at the local library, from a friend, at a Career Centre – and go there. Get as much information as possible in order to make an informed decision.

Decision time: Now that you have a good list of possibilities, it's time to make some decisions. Remember that you may have to take things in stages. You can set short-term and long-term goals. For example, decide to take a broadcasting course in the short-term if your long-term goal is to use your beautiful voice to become a radio personality. Or join a climbing club if your long-term goal is to find several friends who would like to join you in climbing Mount Everest. Or you might lose eight pounds in the next two months if your long-term goal is to lose thirty.

Before you go off to pursue your goals, there are two last steps. First, explore what might prevent you from achieving your goal. Then you can incorporate strategies to deal with these road blocks when you reach the final step in the goal-setting process – developing a plan detailing the specific strategies you have in mind for achieving your goals.

SAMPLE

Setting Goals for my Physical Well-being

I. Me Now

I am:

- 42 years old
- sedentary, hardly get any exercise
- 10 pounds overweight
- unhappy about my body
- going to feel better physically and emotionally when I am at least 5 pounds lighter

I can:

- swim, bike, walk, dance, ski
- diet successfully with Weight Watchers

II. The New Me

In the long-term:

- 10 pounds lighter
- enjoying a regular exercise program
- feeling good about my body
- feeling healthier

In the short-term:

- 5 pounds lighter
- maintaining a regular exercise program
- able to talk with others about dieting
- feeling healthier

III. Decision

I will:

– join Weight Watchers
– lose 5 pounds in the first month
– lose 5 pounds over the next 3 months
– use exercise bike 15 minutes/day at least 4 times/week
– walk with a co-worker at lunch at least twice a week

IV. Barriers I Might Encounter in Getting There

– kids like sweets
– exercise bike is in the basement

V. Strategies to Eliminate or Reduce These Barriers

– ask kids to eat sweets elsewhere and not to ask for them at home
– ask kids to help me move bike to my bedroom

VI. Strategies to Reach My Short-and Long-term Goals

– join Weight Watchers tomorrow
– clear out all sweets and temptations from fridge and cupboards tonight
– buy healthy food after first Weight Watchers' meeting, buy healthy food from now on
– talk to kids about supporting me while dieting
– move bike to my bedroom. Use bike in the morning on weekends and Monday and Wednesday
– arrange with Gloria and/or Julie to walk with me at lunch on Tuesdays and Thursdays
– reward myself with a manicure when I lose the first 5 pounds
– reward myself with a new dress for work when I lose all 10 pounds
– reward myself with a new outfit for the Christmas party when I have kept the 10 pounds off for 3 months

Setting Goals
for my
Physical Well-being

I. Me Now

II. The New Me

In the long-term (List all possibilities):

In the short-term (List all possibilities):

III. Decision

IV. Barriers I Might Encounter in Getting There

V. Strategies to Eliminate or Reduce These Barriers

VI. Strategies to Reach My Short- and Long-term Goals

SAMPLE

Setting Goals for My Emotional Well-being

I. *Me now*

I am:

- recently divorced from my wife
- feeling alienated, lonely, isolated
- sad and guilty because my relationship with my children is distant
- feeling unable to care for myself

I can:

- work at developing a closer relationship with my children
- make friends
- learn to take care of myself

II. *The New Me*

In the long-term:

- have a meaningful and fulfilling relationship with my children
- have friends to share things with and spend time with
- be independent and confident that I can look after myself

In the short-term:

- develop one friend
- begin to work on re-establishing a relationship with my children
- decide what I could do to create a comfortable home for myself
- learn how to cook

III. Decision

I will:

– phone the kids at least twice a week and invite them over at least once a week

– buy a cookbook

– buy food regularly and learn to cook three healthy meals

– put up pictures on the walls of my apartment

– buy a comfortable chair for the living room

IV. Barriers I Might Encounter in Getting There

– feeling uncomfortable talking to the kids on the phone

– worrying that I will be a burden to my friends and that I have nothing to offer them

– working long hours to avoid going home to a lonely apartment

– eating all my meals out because it's easier

V. Strategies to Eliminate or Reduce These Barriers

– accept that I'll feel uncomfortable and call the kids anyway

– list all the positive things that I have to offer to a friendship

– spend at least two waking hours a day in my apartment

– eat at least one meal a day at home

VI. Strategies to Reach My Short- and Long-term Goals

– call my kids on Tuesdays and Sundays

– call Gord this week and ask him if he would like to get together this weekend

– go to a bookstore on the weekend and ask for help in selecting a cookbook

– choose a recipe from my cookbook and make at least one meal

- look in the paper to see if there are any cooking classes offered in the near future
- buy two pictures by the end of next week and hang them
- start looking for the comfortable chair and buy one within two weeks after pay day

Setting Goals
for My
Emotional Well-being

I. Me Now

II. The New Me

In the long-term (List all possibilities):

In the short-term (List all possibilities):

III. *Decision*

IV. *Barriers I Might Encounter in Getting There*

V. *Strategies to Eliminate or Reduce These Barriers*

VI. *Strategies to Reach My Short- and Long-term Goals*

SAMPLE

Setting Goals
for my
Social Life

I. Me Now

I am:

- 31 and recently divorced
- lost several "couples" friends during and after divorce
- haven't talked to friends from when I was single for years
- very involved with the children
- lonely

I can:

- make friends
- re-learn squash
- enjoy music
- get babysitters

II. The New Me

In the long-term:

- with an enlarged circle of friends
- friends with people who can play squash and enjoy music
- not lonely

In the short-term:

- find one or two potential friends
- play squash again
- go to at least one musical event

III. *Decision*

I will:

– find (or reacquaint myself with) some friends
– join a health club or community centre program
– find at leat 2 regular squash partners
– go to music events regularly

IV. *Barriers I Might Encounter in Getting There*

– fear of rejection when trying to make friends
– guilt about leaving kids with babysitter

V. *Strategies to Eliminate or Reduce These Barriers*

– make decision to ignore fear of rejection and make first phone call within 3 days
– arrange to have quality time with kids right before going out
– find trustworthy babysitter that kids like
– enlist support from Mom

VI. *Strategies to Reach My Short- and Long-term Goals*

– call the Arts Centre tomorrow for information about upcoming musical events
– get in touch with 2 old friends by Friday, ask if they'd like to go to a concert sometime, offer to phone the Box Office for tickets
– get information about health clubs/community centres on the weekend and select one by Sunday night, join it on Monday
– ask at club or centre about how to meet squash partners at my level, follow up
– ask at kids' school about babysitters, arrange for him/her to meet kids

- call Mom and ask her for dinner on Wednesday. Ask for her support and suggestions, ask if she'd be willing to babysit now and then
- plan special activity with kids for night before the concert

Setting Goals
for my
Social Life

I. Me Now

II. The New Me

In the long-term (List all possibilities):

In the short-term (List all possibilities):

III. Decision

IV. Barriers I Might Encounter in Getting There

V. Strategies to Eliminate or Reduce These Barriers

VI. Strategies to Reach My Short- and Long-term Goals

Setting Goals for my Spiritual Life

We have chosen not to provide an example of a goal-setting sheet for the spiritual component of your quest. The spiritual side of your life is entirely individual, based on your own values and beliefs. We feel that providing a sample sheet would reflect our beliefs, but would certainly not fit with everyone else's. For ideas about this goal-setting exercise, refer to **Making Meaning** on page 83.

I. Me Now

II. The New Me

In the long-term (List all possibilities):

In the short-term (List all possibilities):

III. Decision

IV. Barriers I Might Encounter in Getting There

V. Strategies to Eliminate or Reduce These Barriers

VI. Strategies to Reach My Short- and Long-term Goals

SAMPLE

Setting Goals
for my
Financial Well-being

I. Me Now

I am:

- recently separated, employed, with one child in my custody
- minimal child support from husband, many missed payments
- no savings or credit rating
- small apartment at reasonable rent
- husband always looked after finances

I can:

- learn how to manage my finances
- learn how to establish a credit rating
- find ways to save
- learn about my legal rights regarding child support

II. The New Me

In the long-term:

- financially secure
- savings for a comfortable retirement
- able to put kids through university or college

In the short-term:

- savings to meet emergencies
- establish an organized system to deal with finances
- establish a credit rating
- regular child support payments coming in

III. Decision

I will:

- go to a financial planning seminar
- get legal advice about child support
- talk to the bank about establishing a credit rating

IV. What Barriers Might I Encounter in Getting There

- feeling overwhelmed and confused about how and where to start in getting organized and getting a credit rating
- worry about causing more fights with my husband
- worry that I'm too broke to save any money and that I'll have to give up smoking

V. Strategies to Eliminate or Reduce These Barriers

- tell myself that I'll take it one day at a time with help from others and from the financial planning workshop
- tell myself that it's my husband's responsibility to help support our child and I deserve that help
- recognize that deciding to look into my financial situation doesn't commit me to any action, including quitting smoking

VI. Strategies to Reach My Short- and Long-term Goals

- make enquiries on Friday about Financial Planning seminars by looking in the newspaper for advertisements, calling my local college or library or talking with friends and co-workers; sign up for a seminar
- phone the nearest Legal Aid office tomorrow to get information about my child support problems
- phone the bank tomorrow to set up an appointment to discuss establishing a credit rating

Setting Goals
for my
Financial Well-being

I. Me Now

II. The New Me

In the long-term (List all possibilities):

In the short-term (List all possibilities):

III. Decision

IV. Barriers I Might Encounter in Getting There

V. Strategies to Eliminate or Reduce These Barriers

VI. Strategies to Reach My Short- and Long-term Goals

SAMPLE

Setting Goals
for my
Career

I. *Me Now*

I am:

- 45 year old school teacher
- committed to my class from now (Oct.) to the end of June
- feeling burned out, bored, overworked, underpaid
- needing a change

I can:

- move because the kids are grown up
- go back to school
- change my job and/or career

II. *The New Me*

In the long-term:

- enjoying my job, feeling stimulated and excited by what I do
- financially secure
- out of the present school

In the short-term:

- having decided on a plan of attack

III. *Decision*

I will:

- review my financial situation
- attend a career decision-making workshop

IV. Barriers I Might Encounter in Getting There

- I'll get scared of failing in my new situation
- I'll get scared about giving up the financial security and stability of my present life

V. Strategies to Eliminate or Reduce These Barriers

- list the positive things to be gained from making a change
- remind myself that this is an exploration of possibilities that doesn't commit me to making a change
- remind myself that I won't give up my regular income until I have a strategy for ensuring my financial security

VI. Strategies to Reach My Short- and Long-term Goals

- go to the library on Saturday and get a book on financial planning which includes a form for reviewing my present situation
- call the nearest Career Planning Centre on Monday and sign up for a career planning workshop

Setting Goals
for my
Career

I. Me Now

II. The New Me

In the long-term (List all possibilities):

In the short-term (List all possibilities):

III. Decision

IV. Barriers I Might Encounter in Getting There

V. Strategies to Eliminate or Reduce These Barriers

VI. Strategies to Reach My Short- and Long-term Goals

A Word about Procrastination

Even in the best of times, many of us procrastinate when faced with unpleasant or overwhelming tasks. During times of high stress, we are often more prone to procrastinate.

What is It?

Procrastination involves putting things off – for an hour, a day, a week or even a lifetime. It's a habit and it usually makes us feel bad.

Why Do We Do It?

Procrastination is actually a coping strategy – not a very successful one, we'll grant you, but definitely a coping strategy. People who procrastinate are usually attempting to cope with unpleasant feelings by avoiding the things that make them feel anxious.

Take, for example, the divorced woman who is avoiding doing her first solo income tax submission. Perhaps she fears that by completing the task she will have to confront the fact that she is now truly on her own. Or she may fear that she will be successful. She may feel that this evidence of her competence may prove to her friends that she can survive and she will no longer feel able to call on them to help her through this difficult period. There are many motivations for procrastination, but they can normally be traced back to some fear that we don't want to confront.

What are the Consequences?

Normally, there are two kinds of consequences. First, we experience distress – an internal consequence. We berate ourselves for not completing the task and resolve to do better next time. If we fail to complete the task again, the feelings of inadequacy intensify. And so it goes, in a downward spiral, sometimes to despair and self-loathing.

The second set of consequences is external. Procrastination may result in small or large consequences depending on the circumstances – being late because a blouse needed ironing, losing a promotion because a job was done poorly at the last minute or losing a friend because commitments were broken.

In the case of the missed income tax deadline, the woman will either lose money because she is penalized for late payment or she will not receive money to which she's entitled because she isn't able to notify the government she is due a refund.

She may also worry about it on a daily basis. Frequently, the internal consequences (worry, self-loathing, increasing stress) are actually far graver than the external consequences.

What to Do?

If you are a procrastinator, there are a number of steps you can take to try to turn things around.

First, ask yourself what your procrastination patterns are. Normally people procrastinate in one or two areas of their life. Finances and organization of the household are two common areas.

Next, try to determine why you procrastinate. What do you gain by procrastinating? What would happen if you stopped? Sometimes simply understanding why you do it helps in breaking the procrastination habit.

Now ask yourself what you do when you are procrastinating. Do you watch television? Clean the house? Drink? Eat? Play solitaire? Find out what behaviors you engage in when you are busy avoiding what you feel you ought to be doing.

Finally, set reasonable goals for yourself. Decide on a course of action that will result in a reduction of the procrastinating behaviors. Remember that procrastinators are often perfectionists! It will be tempting to set impossible goals. (*I will never procrastinate again.*) Instead, set yourself a goal that will make you feel good because it's easier to achieve. (*By Tuesday, I will collect together all the papers I need to get started on my income tax.*)

By exploring why and how you procrastinate, you will gain valuable insights into your actions. Using these insights to set small, reasonable goals will help you manage your procrastinating behaviors.

Assessing Your Areas of Procrastination

Under each main heading, identify your problem areas. Then place an "X" on the lines to indicate the severity of the consequences – both internally (how it makes you feel) and externally (what are the actual results). Once you have completed this assessment, you will have a clearer idea of what needs doing in order to break the procrastination habit.

Home (e.g. yard maintenance, house cleaning, etc.)

My problem areas:

Internal Consequences

Mild   Moderate   Severe

External Consequences

Mild   Moderate   Severe

Personal Care (e.g. losing weight, making long-term life decisions, etc.)

My problem areas:

Internal Consequences

Mild   Moderate   Severe

External Consequences

Mild   Moderate   Severe

Finances (e.g. balancing your cheque book, doing income tax, etc.)

My problem areas:

Internal Consequences

_____

Mild   Moderate   Severe

External Consequences

_____

Mild   Moderate   Severe

Social Relationships (e.g. personal correspondence, confronting someone with a problem, etc.)

My problem areas:

Internal Consequences

_____

Mild   Moderate   Severe

External Consequences

_____

Mild   Moderate   Severe

Other (_____)

My problem areas:

Internal Consequences

_____

Mild   Moderate   Severe

External Consequences

Mild	Moderate	Severe

Other (_____)

My problem areas:

Internal Consequences

Mild	Moderate	Severe

External Consequences

Mild	Moderate	Severe

$\mathcal{R}$esources

Relationships

Barbach, Lonnie Garfield. *For Each Other: Sharing Sexual Intimacy*. New York: Doubleday and Co., 1982.

Beck, Aaron T. *Love is Never Enough*. New York: Harper and Row, 1988.

Colgrove, M. H. Bloomfield, and P. McWilliams. *How to Survive the Loss of a Love*. New York: Bantam, 1976.

Fisher, Bruce. *Rebuilding: When Your Relationship Ends*. St. Louis Obispo, CA: Impact, 1989.

Krantzler, M. *Creative Divorce*. New York: Signet Books, 1975.

Tatebaum, Judy. *The Courage to Grieve: Recovery and Growth through Grief*. New York: Harper and Row, 1980.

Vaughan, Diane. *Uncoupling: Turning Points in Intimate Relationships*. New York: Vintage Books, 1990.

Waterstein, J. S. and J. B. Kelly. *Surviving the Breakup: How Children and Parents Cope with Divorce*. New York: Basic Books Inc., 1980.

Wylie, Betty Jane. *Beginnings: A Book for Widows*. Toronto: McClelland and Stewart, 1977.

Relaxation and Stress Management

Barlow, D. H. and M. G. Creski. *Mastery of Your Anxiety and Panic Attacks*. New York: Grey Winds Publications, 1989.

Benson, H. *Beyond the Relaxation Response*. New York: Berkley Books, 1984.

Davis, M., E. R. Eskelman and M. McKay. *The Relaxation and Stress Reduction Workbook*. Oakland, CA: New Harbinger Publications, 1988.

Henley, Arthur. *Phobias: The Crippling Fears*. New York: Avon Books, 1987.

Self-Development

Barbach, Lonnie Garfield. *For Yourself: The Fulfilment of Female Sexuality*. New York: Doubleday and Co., 1975.

Broder, Michael. *The Art of Living Single*. New York: Avon Books, 1988.

Bruckner-Gordon, Fredda, Barbara Kuerer Gangi and Geraldine Urbach Wallman. *Making Therapy Work: Your Guide to Choosing, Using and Ending Therapy*. New York: Harper & Row, 1988.

Burns, David D. *The Feeling Good Handbook*. New York: William Morrow and Company Inc., 1989.

Dowling, Colette. *The Cinderella Complex: Womens' Hidden Fear of Independence*. New York: Paper Jacks Ltd., 1981.

Farrell, Warren. *Why Men Are the Way They Are*. New York: Berkley Books, 1986.

Friedman, Sonya. *Smart Cookies Don't Crumble: A Modern Womans' Guide to Living and Loving Her Own Life*. New York: G. P. Putnam & Son, 1985.

Friel, John C. and Linda D. Friel. *Adult Children: The Secrets of Dysfunctional Families*. Pompano Beach, FL: Health Communications, 1988.

Friel, John C. and Linda D. Friel. *An Adult Child's Guide to What is "Normal"*. Deerfield Beach, FL: Health Communications, 1990.

Hyatt, C. and L. Gottleib. *When Smart People Fail*. New York: Penguin Books, 1987.

Lorner, H .G. *The Dance of Intimacy*. New York: Harper and Row, 1985.

Seskin, Jane. *Alone Not Lonely: Independent Living for Women Over Fifty*. Washington, DC: American Association of Retired Persons, 1985.

Shakar, Lynn. *Living Alone and Liking It*. Beverly Hills, CA: Stratford Press Inc., 1981.

Sher, B. *Wishcraft: How to Get What You Really Want*. New York: Ballantine Books, 1979.

Smith, M. J. *When I Say No I Feel Guilty*. Toronto: Bantam Books, 1975.

Stallone, James and Linda Stallone. *On Your Own*. Dallas, PA: Upsheer Press, 1991.

Wylie, Betty Jane. *Successfully Single: How to Live Alone and Like It*. Toronto: Key Porter Books Ltd., 1986.

Zilbergeld, Bernie. *Male Sexuality*. New York: Bantam Books, Inc., 1978.

Self-Esteem

Branden, N. *How To Raise Your Self-Esteem*. Toronto: Bantam Books, 1987.

Corkhill-Briggs, D. *Celebrate Yourself*. Toronto: Doubleday, 1977.